I Dream of a World

I Dream of a World

The Story of a Radical Engineer

Berenice Nyland

PUNCHER & WATTMANN

© Berenice Nyland 2024

This book is copyright. Apart from any fair dealing for the purposes of study and research, criticism, review or as otherwise permitted under the Copyright Act, no part may be reproduced by any process without written permission. Inquiries should be made to the publisher.

First published in 2024
Published by TF
PO Box 279
Waratah NSW 2298

NATIONAL
LIBRARY
OF AUSTRALIA

A catologue record for this book is available from The National Library of Australia.

ISBN   9780646709536

Cover design by David Musgrave
Printed by Lightning Source International

Dedicated to Don Atkinson
15 January 1927 – 10 April 2007

The true scientist, while he may know a great many things that electricity will do, will not attempt to say precisely what electricity is. He knows that our present knowledge, real though it is, is only a part of what there is to know. James Wilson (*Science and the progress of man. 1945*)

Acknowledgements

My sister Margaret must be the first acknowledged. She has read the drafts of this book and made useful comments throughout. She has also been the most amazing research assistant ever. Suddenly remembering where documents are, finding memorabilia from my parents and being prepared to spend lots on postage to send over the treasures she was able to locate. Without her this project would not have reached fruition.

Many people are mentioned in the book. Where possible I have contacted them to gain permission to quote them. All have been amazingly generous and supportive of the book. There are too many to list and I thank you all. People who are now involved in some of the work Don left behind have been supportive and provided valuable information.

Lastly husband Chris deserves a mention as being generally helpful and providing technical support when adjusting to a new computer and clearing paper jams from the printer.

I acknowledge there may be mistakes when describing some of the technical information and all mistakes are mine.

Contents

Chapter 1. Introduction — 9

Chapter 2. Background — 22

Chapter 3. Early influences — 39

Chapter 4. Armidale — 55

Chapter 5. Ghana — 73

Chapter 6. The Flinders years — 90

Chapter 7. The Australian electric car — 106

Chapter 8. Nigerian experiences — 122

Chapter 9. Involvement in Aboriginal struggles — 142

Chapter 10. Supporting the Gurindji land rights struggle — 157

Chapter 11. Post university days — 176

Chapter 12. The bookcase at the end of the life — 193

Chapter 1 — Introduction

This book is about my father Don Atkinson. Don was an electrical engineer, a life-long learner who would move between industry, universities and self-employment throughout his life. He was involved in many historic projects and had an exciting life. His engineering and politics defined him and gave him the means to be an active part of many of the causes that were dear to him. He was caught up in a variety of exciting developments, a proponent of alternative energy, part of Australia's initiative to develop an electric car fifty years ago, an anti-war, anti-nuclear protester, a political activist who worked with the Gurindji of Daguragu and actively supported post-colonial efforts in West Africa. Don's story is part of the history of post-war Australia and has relevance today as we struggle with climate change, a nuclear threat and have no strong policies to promote electric cars in this country. Don would have liked his story told as history was important to him, he had a strong sense of the value of history and what we can learn from our own narratives. At his mother's funeral, a few days before she turned 100, in 2001, he told the assembled family, "I want to explain the century my mother lived through." It was a large funeral as members of the extended family had travelled to Adelaide for the one hundredth birthday. After Don's comment many of the older members of the family wanted a turn to talk about life in the 20th century. The woman at the funeral parlour had told Don he could take his time as there were no more funerals scheduled for the day. The speeches at my grandmother's funeral took many hours. Don's grandson commented afterwards that he had learnt a lot of history.

Don lived through interesting times. In his life he experienced the depression, world war, too many other wars, revolutions and the cold war. It was a period of the beginning of post-colonialism and a flourishing of the sciences, especially physics. With this golden age of physics came the spectre of the bomb. Other movements were growing. The book *Silent Spring* by Rachel Carson in 1962 was the start of a serious worldwide conservation movement. These were all to have a fundamental impact on Don's life. He was a talented electrical engineer, full of energy, love of people, a larger than life figure. He had endless enthusiasm. His adventures not only led him to West Africa, Daguragu (Wattie Creek) and convening one of the first electric car projects in Australia but to involvement in local activism for endless causes.

My mother's dying words were, "I suppose Don was happy." I knew what she meant. He belonged to a particular class of Australian men from the post-world-war-two era. Frenetic in his activities, always wanting to change the world, he never gave up. He was at the edge of many historical events. Technological advances during the war led to numerous developments. By the end of the war he was involved in radar research and this would have far reaching effects from changed cooking habits (the microwave) to more precise meteorology as well as making it possible for Don to be involved in the progress being made in radio-physics and solid-state plasma research. In this book I describe many of his activities and explore the choices he made. He felt driven to be a force for the common good and he had a definite idea of what the common good was. He left school at fifteen and home shortly afterwards and by the time he was a young adult he had a well-developed world view. He was radical but his approach changed from joining the Communist Party of Australia (CPA) as an enthusiastic teenager to applying a more considered Marxist lens to his life-long political and scientific activities. His politics and his engineering were intertwined. He was a mercurial character who cultivated strong friendships, was extremely loyal and managed to maintain a loving family through various scrapes and adventures. An only child he left school in 1942 to take up an apprenticeship. This was war time and the period he lived through helped to drive many of his life's activities.

When Don completed his apprenticeship, he continued to study and developed skills in creative design in his engineering work. He worked in industry and universities, achieving an Australian Research Council linkage grant (ARC) many years after he had left university life and was in his 70s. The ARC project was a collaboration to design and produce a more cost-effective brushless motor through innovative design. An example of his seemingly endless activity was that he managed to be co-author on a paper on the motor he had designed a year after he died.[1] Exploring my father's life is to ask questions about the connections between the age he was born into, his political radicalism and his belief in science? He was an admirer of C.P. Snow who said of the scientists:

> For the future is in our hands, if we care enough. The means exist for our seeing to it that the poor of the world don't stay poor. The scientific and technical knowledge which we now possess is enough, if we can find the human means, to solve the problem within a couple of generations. I do not pretend that it is going to be easy to find the human means-but the knowledge exists and since it exists, no man of the faintest imagination or good will can rest easy.[2]

Don never rested easy. As a young communist in 1951 he wrote an article about the role of the scientist in society. Large parts of this document were political polemic. At that time, he saw the world clearly as good and evil, capitalist and workers, left and right. He also expressed a belief in the capabilities and potential of science and the responsibility scientists had to society. The idea of responsibility was tempered by world events. After Hiroshima and Nagasaki were bombed in 1945 Don became a peace activist. As his electrical engineering skills grew, he became increasingly interested in the environment and sources of alternative energy. Many of his ideas seem prescient in retrospect.

Don was born in 1927, the only child from a working-class family in Western Sydney. Both sides of the family had ancestors who had migrated, or been sent as convicts, from the United Kingdom. His father and mother's families could trace their connection to European Australia back to the early 1800s. The family lived by a canal in Belfield where Don's maternal grandfather, John Whatmough, a tanner, had given Don's parents a block of land to build a house. The older Whatmoughs lived near Don's family home. His paternal grandparents died before he was born. His maternal grandfather was an elegant looking man, slim and 6ft 4ins. He ran his tannery and had a reputation as a binge drinker. He would disappear for a week or so and then reappear in a sorry state. Don's wife, Daphne, said he was very charming. He died in 1954 in his mid-90s and she said weeks before he died he would "still go to the club and flirt with the ladies".

Don had a religious upbringing as his father, David Atkinson, was religious without being particularly public about his beliefs. David was a serious Mason. Don's mother, Annie Atkinson, was neither particularly religious nor strong about the Masons and she treated being a member of the Eastern Star as an enjoyable social commitment. She thoroughly enjoyed her euchre nights with 'the ladies'. The only religious inclination she ever showed was in her early 90s when she started going to church for a while. My son, who was twelve at the time observed the new phenomena and asked why his great grandmother was suddenly going to church. Don, who had a quirky sense of humour said, "Haven't you heard of insurance Morgan". Orphan cousins came to live in the house when Don was in his early teens and with one of his cousins he developed a taste for jazz, they both played trumpet, which was his personal preference for music all his life. After he left home there were stories of leather jackets and motor bikes and when he married he had a motor bike with a side-car.

Having left school at fifteen and completed his apprenticeship as a scientific instrument maker Don went on to a variety of jobs and was a life-long learner. He studied all his life. The family found a student card among his papers dated four years before he died. He was 76 and doing a Technical and Further Education (TAFE) course in computer aided design (CAD) at the time. As he added qualifications and experience to his curriculum vitae he went on to work in physics departments in universities in Australia and West Africa, have his own consultation companies and do one-off design and repair work. By combining his love of electronics with political activism he was able to make choices that led to a busy and fulfilling life and gave an edge to his involvement to save the world that was practical and unusual.

As a communist in the 1950s he was a target of the Australian Security Intelligence Organisation (ASIO). His security rating with ASIO threatened his employment opportunities in Australian universities. It was because of ASIO he found himself at the University of New England with academics and communists like the historian Russell Ward and the labour historian Eric Fry. The University of New England appointed staff on meritocratic grounds and was not vulnerable to government pressure to refuse employment to those who had adverse security ratings. A family connection who had known Don in Armidale came to his funeral in Adelaide. The friend said he thought the reason that Don's stories about discrimination during the cold war were not more widely known was because he was an engineer. The other 'seditious thinkers' in the Armidale group had been social scientists and their stories became well known. Russell Ward because of his book, *The Australian legend,* was famous. Eric Fry became renowned in labour history circles. Another in the group appointed at the time remained in Armidale and became part of the local community. Don, as an engineer, was on the outside. He worked with many radical scientists over the years but there was and is, a divide between the scientists, social scientists and even scientists and engineers.

There are many stories to tell about Don. As a person with left-wing politics he was involved in the folk revival of the 1950s, was a ranger protecting the NSW national parks, worked on alternative energy projects and became an advocate for solar and wind power as early as the 1960s. He was a unionist, a communist for many years and dedicated a decade to supporting the Gurindji struggle for land rights. He was an ardent admirer of Kwame Nkrumah and went to post-colonial Ghana to work with a renowned English physicist who had worked on the Manhattan project in Canada and been jailed for giving atomic research secrets to the Soviet Union. Don worked intermittently in Northern Nigeria between 1966 and the mid-1980s.

He enjoyed life, could be outrageous, often the life of the party, loved music and literature, was amazingly generous and always enthusiastic. Don lived a big life during an historical period that will soon be a distant memory. This book is based on accounts my father kept including letters, official and personal, minutes of meetings, campaign materials, financial records, newspaper cuttings, journal articles, newsletters, personal memories and his ASIO files. Where possible I have researched names and places mentioned, especially as a lack of dates on much of the correspondence has been a problem. Letter writing was a popular protest activity that both my parents engaged in. Undated letters with no envelopes were particular problems but blue aerogram letters sent fortnightly from West Africa were great as they had the post office date stamp on them.

Some of the events Don was a part of have been extensively recorded elsewhere, for instance, the Wave Hill strike by the Gurindji[3] while other endeavours he pursued were unique. Where there are already records in the public domain, like the Gurindji struggle at Daguragu, I have tried to add to existing stories. In this case I found that the Adelaide contribution to the struggle was almost totally missing from the accounts even though the Adelaide group gave significant assistance in the years 1971-1976. There were many activist groups involved in supporting the Gurindji land rights struggle. It was agreed among the numerous support groups that the fight belonged to the Gurindji and supporters from the South needed to work out how to be effective 'do-gooders'.[4] Practices of the Adelaide Gurindji group were carefully developed to give agency to the Gurindji in terms of following advice about assistance needed and making sure the Gurindji were the decision makers in how funds raised would be used. This included informing supporters, who were donating money, that the funds would be used as decided by the Gurindji group and this would entail cash injections to support daily life in times of hardship when the Gurindji were struggling against a hostile welfare system.

As a radical during the cold war era Don's security rating with ASIO impacted on his job opportunities in the 1950s. As well as my own memories and talking to remaining members of the family and friends, I thought a good place to start researching his life would be ordering his ASIO files. When I received Don's files they came in an attractive folder with the words, "Your story, our history" written across the cover. The idea of those words is important even though the contents were pretty much a waste of time. "Your story, our history" does inspire the question, why write a biography? Is the story worth telling? The historical story that is represented in the telling of Don's life contains unique aspects of experience that are important for our understanding of ourselves as a country. These ideas and more are encapsulated in the ASIO motto. Can we learn about social values that help explain our world and the shape of people's lives at particular moments? Can we get a sense of opportunities missed by seeing the paths that were taken by individuals and governments? What did the historical context look like from different perspectives? The surrounding circumstances of Don's life make an interesting story and include larger questions of morality and ethics. A biography of Don's life gives a glimpse of history from a particular perspective. His involvement in certain events was coloured by his childhood, education, personal attraction to left-wing politics, a hatred of racism and a passion for science and ideas.

It was a combination of politics and his science that took him to Ghana in 1964. It was also both these passions that gave him his lifelong antipathy to the World Bank, the International Monetary Fund (IMF) and other such institutions as he became demoralised about the way foreign aid is manipulated to keep countries poor. He became a critic of the Soviet Union when he observed the type of aid being given to the newly independent Ghana and saw it as exploitative. When he came back to Australia, after his first stint in West Africa, he found the Communist Part of Australia (CPA) did not want to hear his ideas on the role of the Soviet Union in Africa. He gradually drifted away from the party. He remained a Marxist, a friend of the left but ceased to be a card-carrying member.

He was an enormously energetic person who sometimes tilted at windmills, real and metaphoric. He could be ahead of his times and aware of past injustices and wrongs that needed to be set to rights. He had heroes, some for life and some had feet of clay. When the latter proved to be the case he could move on without losing his impetus to change the world. Those he genuinely admired, like Professor Jack Somerville, his manager at the University of New England, he would refer back to all his life. Jack Somerville died suddenly at the age of fifty-two and Don kept a portrait of him in his study/workshop for the rest of his life. His loyalties ran deep.

This book is organised chronologically where possible but also by theme. Chapter two provides family background and places worked in a logical succession. Chapter three then introduces some of the influences he encountered on leaving home that would assist in his scientific career and the formation of his attitudes and view of his times. The rest of the book is a mix of chronological events, work, political activity and retirement, which was as busy as the rest of his life. It was a full life well-lived.

As background to the book I have thought about the defining features of Don's character and approach to life that provide the canvas for the activities he participated in. He would throw himself into whatever interest or cause, he decided to pursue. An example of this energy was his relationship with the Labor Party. He was not a member of the Labor Party but at times decided that the opposing Liberal Party was so bad that everyone needed to put all their efforts into helping the Labor Party get elected. This was the case when he was anxious the Whitlam government should get re-elected following 'the dismissal'. He went door knocking and the stories were myriad from mad dogs to naked householders. One house he went to and knocked. A tremulous voice said, "There's no one home". Don's response was to say comfortingly, "All right I'll come back later". He got badly mauled by a dog during his door knocking activities and when he went home he insisted on taking off his outer clothes and washing all the blood off himself with the garden hose before he went inside. He did not want to cause trouble by leaving bloodstains around.

His love of electronics stretched to many different activities. One interest he enjoyed was the design of small parts of a machine. He did some work on the switches on the pedestrian lights at street crossings in Adelaide at one stage. He was impressed at the initial design which had the aim of being vandal proof. This interest in switches led to him designing one-off controls to fit the capacity of an individual user of a mechanism, from a wheelchair to a child's electric train set. One of the companies he set up in his post university days was with my brother-in-law, Kim. They specialised in fixing electric wheelchairs. They found a challenge with wheelchairs was that there were often not enough of the same type to make maintenance easy. Many wheelchairs had distinctive features that made them a one-off. This was not a good environment in which to get speedy repairs. Don and Kim knew that a chair bound person would be limited without their chair so each chair was attended to quickly when it arrived at the workshop. They would also use innovative measures if parts were not available in Australia. This was not a rare occurrence. As Don said, some people had expensive one-off 'rolls royce' wheelchairs, perhaps supplied by a group like Rotary, but there might be only a few in the whole country. This made parts and mending them problematic. His wheelchair involvement included motor design, research on batteries and charges and electrical repairs. Don's skills in designing and building switches to suit individual capacities helped a number of their clients. His work on electric cars and alternative energy had also given him invaluable experience into the potential of batteries which were integral to the working of electric wheelchairs.

Figure 1.1 Don testing a wheelchair in the local park with Bruce the rescue dog

Along with switches and batteries, computers were an important part of Don's life. He used to laugh at the advertisements that suggested they were a must have in the home and you could do wonderful things with them, like catalogue your books and records, balance the household budget (that was for him), store dinner party recipes so you would always give guests something new (that was for her).He had been familiar with computers for most of his working life but did not see the sense of a home computer. For all that he was one of the first I knew to succumb. In the early 1980s he arrived home from Singapore with an Apple 11e clone.

He had a few games on the computer and this was a new experience for the family. One was the maze game "dung beetle" which might have come with the computer as he bought the computer about the time the "dung beetle" game was released. Another was a choose your own adventure, I can't remember the name but it was rather clever. It was a game that seemed specifically designed for the grandchildren. In the game a little man was living on his own and if he did the right things he could gradually expand his household to have a dog, play music, and a friend could visit. I think it must have been an earnest early attempt to get children to be responsible. For example, if the little man forgot to feed the dog it would die. I can't remember how he could get the dog to come back to life. Each time the game was turned on it would start from where the last game had been played. These were the days when people wrote their own code so Don turned his hand at trying to design a game as well. I can't remember any details now but it was a maze, like "dung beetle", and he was pleased with it.

In the late 1980s Don had a stroke. He underwent rehabilitation for about a year and part of this was speech therapy. All his life he had a slight lisp. He could not pronounce 'th'. He would say 'three' as 'free'. After his rehabilitation his lisp was gone. This was slightly disquieting. He was left with a paralysed right hand and although he had always had a dominant left hand he had trouble writing. He developed all sorts of ways of trying not to make his frozen hand obvious. He loved having people around for drinks and would always be mine host. Moving around the room filling up glasses he was in his element. If you had just arrived he would ask what you wanted, come back with an appropriate glass tucked into his right arm and a bottle in the left. He would use his left hand to pass the glass and then pour the drink. He got very good at these types of manoeuvres. My mother, Daphne, could not drive so after the stroke he needed to buy an automatic car and work out how to turn the steering wheel. Daphne made a sling and attached it to the steering wheel of the car. Don could put his right hand in the sling and would use the weight of his hand to turn the wheel. When he was organising a new car, he needed to sell his old one. He rang and asked if I could still do his signature. I had been out of school for some twenty years and never suspected he knew I used to sign the school report cards for my sister, Mayo and myself. More importantly, he was able to adopt the new voice recognition programs available for computers. He was one of the first people I had seen use the technology. He was able to continue with his design work even though he could now only use one hand.

Don could be a trickster. The automatic car he bought was a Toyota. Coming home one day he noticed Kim, my brother-in-law, had parked his Toyota in front of the house and it was not locked. He had a quick brain flip, popped into the car and sure enough his key fitted and the car started. He managed to drive it around the corner so that Kim would come out and think his car had been stolen. Not sure that Kim was amused.

Don was also the human embodiment of John Williamson's song "All Australian boys need a shed". The first house he bought in Adelaide had a garage. By the time he finished it had a second garage in front of the first and a studio attached to the original garage. When he moved across town he was in shed heaven because he had a big yard that could house a number of sheds without being too obvious and my grandmother moved from Sydney to a house just up the road. Her new house had a workshop and sheds. He almost burnt a shed at my grandmother's house down once. He left some papers and his glasses on the bench. The sun was just at the right angle. Luckily someone noticed as the paper was turning brown and the smoke was beginning to rise.

There are plenty of anecdotes about my father, the places he went, the people he knew and the work he did. Many are quite funny and have become family legends. Like his statement at my grandmother's funeral this is my offering of the time he lived through. My mother's last words about supposing Don was happy were bitter/sweet. Given his belief in people and life it would have been easy to become depressed when there seemed to be many failures along the road. The world he wanted to build was never to be but he never lost the spirit to keep trying. He had a strong imagination which could be a source of trouble. During the Iraq war he became intensely disturbed about the lack of reporting of civilian deaths and injuries. He started trying to keep his own records by taping news reports each day and trying to combine them. My older sister died in 2006. The family was devastated. Don spoke to me about his feelings one night. He was experiencing guilt. We could have the luxury of our outpouring of grief in the safety of our own homes. The idea that the death of each Iraqi was equally as distressing to their families was one he could not get out of his head. He could feel overwhelmed with such thoughts.

He was always keen to share his ideas. Each Christmas he would present everyone with a book with a 'life lesson' in it. Sometimes these were brief. As my son was going into high school, in 1993, he gave him a copy of John Gribbin's, *Hothouse earth: the greenhouse effect and Gaia*. The brief message read, "enhanced greenhouse may turn out to be hot-air. John Gribbin's account of climate processes is connected with everyday experiences; fun to read". Like many of his scientific compatriots Einstein was a giant to him. In 1979 he gave my husband, Chris, Nigel Calder's, *Einstein's universe*. The message he wrote sums up his enthusiasm:

> To honour a man such as Albert Einstein was – and to reverence his memory, is to suggest that we would and will try to make more and better use of our own time and capabilities.
> Einstein formulated his exquisite creative theories and aesthetic equations of matter while working alone, with paper and pencil, chalk and eraser. It is likely that had he tons of technicians working with him, and banks of computers, those would have proved to be hindrances to his creative endeavours.

He enjoyed looking at life through the lens of those he admired and if they were enthusiasts his pleasure was greater. In 2001 he gave my sister, Margaret, Oliver Sacks', *Uncle Tungsten: Memories of a chemical boyhood.* He wrote a message and then included a review from the *New York Times* by Erica Goode.[5] He wrote: "We try to buy books that the recipient will like, but the giver has their bias. Trust you enjoy Uncle Tungsten, Love Dad". The review summed up his feelings about the book. When asked by the reviewer why this book seemed different from other Oliver Sacks books Sacks said he was not sure. He thought a parcel from a friend with a small bar of tungsten in it started him thinking.

> It brought to mind my Uncle Tungsten, with his wing collar and his tungsten-blackened hands. And then other things came to me and other things.
> I found myself very divided between personal history and the history of chemistry, although in a way they seem to come naturally together and not to be artificially yoked, because I was partly living through some of the history of chemistry. I didn't start with up-to-date textbooks but with my uncles' early Victorian books.

When asked if he had left any of the elements out of the book Sacks replied, "I like them all". My father had this kind of enthusiasm for life, living and electronics.

Chapter 2 Background

Annie Irene Whatmough married David George Atkinson on the 11th April 1925. David worked as an electro plater at AWA (Amalgamated Wireless Australasia) for most of his working life. He died at work of a heart attack in 1963. Annie was a housewife who went to work in the railway yards (Enfield marshalling yards) near their home in Belfield in the early days of world-war-two. Her main occupation was sewing tarpaulins. She would work there until the 1950s.

Figure 2.1 Don's parents on their wedding day

Donald Alfred Atkinson was born on the 15th January 1927. He was an only child. He had a sister June who died soon after her birth. When he was a teenager two cousins, Vern and Bill Whatmough, on his mother's side, lost their parents. Vern and Bill came to live with the Atkinsons. Vern went on to do an apprenticeship as a boilermaker and Bill joined the army. Don went to a local primary school and then to Canterbury Boys High School and then did an apprenticeship with Braybon Brothers where he qualified as a scientific instrument maker. His parents were disappointed as they had wanted him to complete high school and go on to study for a profession. Both his parents had left school at the end of their primary education and had wanted more for their son.

The family home was in Blanche Street, Belfield. Annie's father had been a tanner and had his business at the back of Blanche Street by a canal that linked to the Cook River. Looking at maps of historical waterways of Sydney I think it could be the Cox Creek channel. Annie's father owned a large piece of land by the canal and gave blocks of land to his children as they married. Annie and David built their home on the land John Whatmough had gifted to them. The home Annie and David built was to be Annie's home until she was in her mid-eighties. She had been widowed in 1963 and in 1985 Annie moved to Adelaide to be closer to Don as she aged. Annie and David were solid working-class people who enjoyed sport and participated in community activities. Annie was a tennis player who moved onto bowls when tennis became too strenuous. She helped found the local bowls club and became president of this club, the Belfield Bowls Club, in the 1970s. David was a Mason and keen on the scout movement. His father had run a laundry business in Strathfield.

Don used to tease his mother by telling tall stories about growing up in the depression. He would tell us children about starving, going to school in bare feet in the middle of winter and add lots of gruesome details. His mother would get really annoyed with him and tell us these things never happened. She never learnt though and he could get a rise out of her every time he decided to tell tall stories. One of our favourite stories was that because he was an only child and his parents doted on him so much, they decided to give him 29 names to show how important he was. He would reel off 29 names every time we asked for the story. I don't know how much they changed with each telling but my sister, Margaret and I remember the first four distinctly; "Donald, Alfred, King George, Aloysius.

Figure 2.2 Don 11 years

Home life was organised and calm. Don was in the scouts, learnt music, there were a few books in the house. I still have his copy of *The Children's Treasure House* that he was given when he was 8 or 9. He took pleasure in introducing his own children to this book and all our families have facsimile copies of the original. Growing up he had plenty of friends but by the time he had a family of his own, except for the cousins, Vern and Bill, most of his friends came from his post school days. Annie was the matriarch of the family so festivals like Christmas dinner were held at Belfield and various members of the extended family would gather. Vern married and stayed in Sydney so his family was a fixture at family gatherings. Bill came back to visit when he was first in the army but when he married he moved to North Queensland and contact was mainly through birthday and Christmas cards. He died of a heart attack in his early 40s.

Because David worked at AWA the family were one of the first in the street to get a television. The television arrived in 1958[1] and was a favourite with all the family. Don and family were living in Armidale when television arrived in Sydney and the TV added spice to Christmas holidays. Don and Annie would watch the tennis together on Saturday afternoons. This was a great joy when we visited the grandparents as Armidale did not get television until the 1960s. By the time TV arrived in Armidale the family had gone overseas. This meant Don did not have access to television in the home until the move to Adelaide in 1966. As it was Don and Daphne decided it was not a healthy obsession and did not get a television until the 1970s. Even then they would not have bothered but when everyone started getting colour television there were lots of black and white sets being given away. They reluctantly accepted their first one but quickly upgraded to colour. The radio, however, remained a major source of news and entertainment throughout their lives.

When Don undertook his apprenticeship at Braybon Brothers he moved away from Belfield and into the city proper. This move created opportunities for a young man keen on music and with a personality that was ready to branch out and embrace the excitement that inner city living had to offer. From Braybon Brothers Don gained an appreciation of machinery and tools and this was the start of his becoming a skilled electrical engineer. While at Braybon Brothers he achieved a Certificate of Trade Competency, for electrical fitters in 1946, a five-year course at Sydney Technical College and graduated with supplementary trade instructions for electrical fitters in January 1947. An Intermediate BSc from London University as an external student followed and in 1951 he completed an Industrial Electronics course at Granville Technical College. He was admitted to the Bachelor of Science at the University of New South Wales in 1956.

Towards the end of the war he was given the chance to work with radar, along with many others and this was a discrete step in his work identity. He was still at Braybon Brothers when he met my mother, Daphne Odora Ockenden, who, at his funeral, reminisced on their life together. She spoke of how they met and married when they had known each other for six weeks.

> We met at the Modern Writer's Club one evening and found we had common interests. He ranged through Philosophy, Politics, History, Music – and his Science and Engineering studies were always his life. Six weeks after this meeting we rather astounded everyone by getting married.

About the time they got married Don had moved to Bunnerong Power Station. At Bunnerong he described his job as centred around repairs to electrical recording and control instruments and assisting in the development of specialised test equipment. It was at Bunnerong that he was exposed to asbestos, finally dying of mesothelioma in 2007. My mother always said he must have had the constitution of an ox for the disease to take so long to affect him.

Figure 2.3 Wedding photo of Daphne Odora Vincent Ockenden and Donald Alfred Atkinson, Easter 1949

Don was working at Bunnerong when my sister Mayo (originally Mao) and I were born. He had moved to Heathcote, south of Sydney in the Sutherland shire, sometime in the early 1950s. He had been living in the city after the war and he and Daphne lived in Kings Cross for a short time together. The move to Heathcote was supported by my maternal grandfather, Roy Ockenden, who helped the young couple to acquire land and assisted in the building of the house at the top of Dillwynia Grove. This was a collaborative move because when the family moved to Canberra grandfather sold his Hurstville house and moved to Heathcote. Roy was there until his death in 1968. Heathcote in the early 1950s had cheap building land available. It was 30 kilometres south of Sydney and serviced twice daily by a steam train on the Illawarra line. Don and

Daphne's house was built at the top of Dillwynia Grove opposite an old mansion called Heathcote Hall.

Daphne, Don and Roy were part of a group of like-minded people with left-wing politics, many in the Communist Party with a love of the Australian bush, who found themselves attracted to Heathcote. Moving there was like old home week as there was an immediate social scene because a number of friends, acquaintances and fellow communists established themselves in Heathcote at the same time. The housing shortage after the war meant people often built their own structures to live in while saving money to build a house. It was not unusual for houses in Heathcote to have garages that had originally been divided into living and sleeping spaces. Our house was modest, it had electricity but no inside toilet. There was an Australian invention called the Hygeia dissolvenator toilet[2] at the bottom of the back yard. Trips down the yard at night were terrifying. I can clearly remember this toilet as it was still in use later when my Grandfather, Roy, was living in the house. An inside toilet was not installed until after Roy died and the house was sold.

The Australian bush, literature, history and music were interests those in Heathcote shared. The folk revival was underway and many proponents of this music were members of the Communist Party, or the Eureka Youth League (EYL). Musicians on the left were collecting songs from the past, Henry Lawson poems were being set to music and community choirs became popular. This enthusiasm for Australian songs of work and struggle was shared by many in Heathcote. It was here in Heathcote that the original Bushwackers band, called the Heathcote Bushwackers, under the leadership of John Meredith, was formed in 1952. It is slightly ironic that some of the original Australian repertoire of the Bushwackers came from the American singer Burl Ives who had introduced songs like *Click Go the Shears* to the Australian public when he toured the country in 1952.

A love of the surrounding bush was something the family enjoyed. Heathcote had great walking tracks around it and a swimming hole not far into the national park from the bottom of Dillwynia Grove (see photo below). Daphne and Don joined the park rangers and took the role of caring for the national park seriously. I can remember going for a Sunday drive in Grandfather's car. Don spotted some people dumping rubbish. He took their number, told them off and waited until they had put the rubbish back in the boot of their car before he would drive off. Another community activity was trapping funnel web spiders to take into a hospital in Sydney so their venom could be milked for an antivenin.

Figure 2.4 The family, 1953, Karloo Pools Heathcote

The years in Heathcote were hectic for the family. Don and Daphne were both working. Don worked in Sydney, moving from his job at Bunnerong to CSIRO (Commonwealth Research and Industry Organisation) as a Technical Assistant with the Wool and Textile Laboratories at Ryde. Daphne, who was a trained nurse, worked in the tuberculosis sanatorium at Waterfall, which was near Heathcote. They were actively involved in political activities, their 1953 ASIO file says they were leading communists in the Heathcote area. Music and youth groups were part of their occupations and they were members of a group called the *Western Sydney Singers*. They managed all this as well as having a young family and a dog, a kelpie cross called Rusty. What they did for childcare I do not know as grandparents were not available. When they moved to Canberra there was a creche but Heathcote and surrounds did not stretch to such a facility. The train went twice a day so Don kept pretty tight work hours only occasionally getting 'stuck' in Sydney when there had been a few drinks at the pub after work.

Figure 2.5 Don Atkinson (on right) with fellow worker at Bunnerong

Don left his Bunnerong job in 1951 and took up his position with the CSIRO. A work letter that exists in the file from this time is from Don querying issues with an infra-red spectrometer and he is asking the company that supplied it if the convexity of the prism faces have been polished correctly as he is having focus problems.

The first real impact of his adverse ASIO rating occurred at this job with CSIRO in early 1952. A letter on the 6th March dismissed him from this position with CSIRO although the writer assures him there is "no need for you to feel any stigma of summary dismissal' only that the position you had been appointed to was pending and "did not develop." Another job around this time seems to have been a brief 7 months at Westinghouse but as Don did not remember this job when he made a list of all the places he had worked it can probably stay forgotten.

After CSIRO Don moved to the Sydney University Medical School as a senior laboratory technician. At Sydney he was involved in work that encompassed both mechanical and electronic engineering. He was responsible for construction and maintenance of equipment that included an infra-red spectrometer for gas analysis, an electron magnetic flow meter and other electro-physiological apparatus. In a job application Don reported that at Sydney University he was responsible for equipment that ranged from microscopes to frequency modulated blood pressure recording devices. It was an exciting time to be an engineer. At Sydney one of his colleagues was a friend and fellow communist, Richard (Dick) Makinson. Makinson was a brilliant physicist with a PhD from Cambridge. He suffered for his political beliefs during the cold war and was denied a chair at Sydney University. Dick Makinson was another of those my father spoke about with admiration and liking all his life.

Figure 2.6 Don at Sydney University 1953

After Sydney University, in 1955, Don went to the John Curtin Medical School in Canberra. A university house was made available. This was usual at the time as Canberra had little housing available and the university made housing available to attract staff. The family had two different addresses in Canberra, both university houses. At the John Curtin Medical School Don was appointed as a Technical Officer Grade 11 (electronics) with a salary of £963 per year. He had been promoted to a Technical Officer Grade 111 when he left in 1957 with a starting salary of £1146 and £35 annual increments to look forward to.

The ANU had a number of social clubs for staff and families. The John Curtin Medical School had established a film group in 1953 and this was extended to all university staff in 1955. The stated object of the film group was to "advance the cultural interest of its members through the medium of films and to educate members in the technological aspect of film craft." The club showed "feature films and films of technical and general interest." Don and Daphne were members of the Canberra Peace Group and one of Don's activities was fundraising. The ANU film group offered a useful venue and there is a letter on file from the secretary allotting certain film nights to Don for the peace group and other nights to people who were raising funds for approved worthy causes.

The ANU was still fairly new when Don started working at the John Curtin Medical School. The first stone for the medical school had been laid by Ben Chiffley in 1949. The university did not start moving into permanent buildings until 1952. As a research university 370 staff out of 470 staff were classified as general staff. This was explained by location and function and helped define the role of technicians in the institution. Unlike Sydney and Melbourne, Canberra did not have a nearby source of workshops and factories where goods could be ordered. The ANU workshops had to make many of their own materials and if goods were brought in from outside storage space and staff were needed. As a research-oriented university the focus of the institution was pure research, as opposed to under-graduate teaching and more assistance from technicians and office staff was required.

By 1956 the general staff were concerned they had no meeting space for the General Staff Association and were looking at alternative means to exchange work-based information. A magazine was established by the group called *Owls and Fowls*. The first edition came out in August 1956 and it was planned to appear at two monthly intervals. There was an editor and two committee members for the magazine. One of the two committee members was Don Atkinson. The building problems mentioned above attracted one letter to the editor and a poem in the first edition of *Owls and Fowls*. A person calling themselves Cato wrote a poem for the magazine that was titled: *On first looking out the window.*

"On first looking out the library window"

An hour-long weary rumble,

> Sounding bored and overhung,
>
> A yellow, ponderous arm,
>
> A fist clenched and then outflung;
>
> Slow movements, awkward, rigid
>
> Grumbling, tense, unsung,
>
> Cold to the touch and dirty –
>
> Made use of by everyone;
>
> Misunderstood, neglected,
>
> Neurotic and highly strung,
>
> The Med. School earth remover
>
> Stays condemned to scooping dung.

Don's work in Canberra seemed to be similar to the responsibilities he had enjoyed in Sydney. He reported that while he had been employed at the John Curtin he was in charge of the electronics laboratory and during his time there he had constructed Geiger counters, ratemeters, a specialised blood-pressure recorder and an automatic recording radio-active chromatogram scanner. This latter was the focus of a paper presented by Dr Blakely at a national conference. What emerges from Don's descriptions of his work was the emphasis on what was built and what was maintained. He was committed to engineering as a practical pursuit. He took pride in machinery, insisted that it was kept in good order and took pleasure in making tools that worked. The same feeling comes across in his explanations of the work he did in Armidale, the electric car group he convened in Adelaide and his explanations of his work in Nigeria at Ahmadu Bello University.

My sister, Margaret, was born in Canberra in 1955. It was in Canberra that ASIO surveillance seems to have been stepped up to the extent of watching the house. Previously the ASIO files had reports from casual spies who picked up gossip or sent copies of minutes of meetings and lists of attendees of meetings to the agency. Now there were people watching the houses. This surveillance occurred at both addresses that the family lived in while in Canberra. The ASIO spies regularly sent lists of cars parked out the front of the house and lists of people who attended meetings and parties. Such lists seem to have been the popular information of the moment. Daphne and Don hosted a lot of political meetings at their own home so maybe that was the reason they were of such interest to the security agents. Daphne used to joke that one cold night she had even taken a cup of tea to the poor person watching the house from their car. One incident, vaguely amusing, was that one of the ASIO spies reported that Don was working on a nuclear project. This created enough kerfuffle for the agency to check this out and to add a special report to his file to say there was no evidence of such work. I do not know where the rumour came from but there is a letter of Don's in the work file asking about scintillation gels and low level C14 counting. The letter was to a company called Canadian Nuclear Enterprise Ltd. Given what his work entailed at the time he was probably enquiring into something to do with x-ray research and the name of the Canadian company might have been enough to startle some over-alert spy.

From Canberra Don moved to Armidale in 1957 and the Armidale story is related in a separate chapter. His time at the medical school in Canberra ended less than happily and there is a letter from the registrar, dated February 28th, 1957, accepting his resignation. It is a short, formal letter with a slightly mysterious middle paragraph.

> I have noted your comments as given in the second paragraph of your letter of resignation but I am glad to know that apart from this you have found your work with the Australian National University satisfying.

We will never know what Don said in his resignation letter but he was certainly included in the group of people employed by the University of New England who had been discriminated against in the 1950s because of their politics. He was always bitter towards some universities as he said they had either sacked him or refused him employment during this period. His reason for eventually going to Adelaide was that Flinders was a new university and he hoped it would be a more open and tolerant environment in which to work than what he had experienced in the cold war era.

The years in Armidale were a period where Don's radical life of politics and science activities seemed to come converge. After Armidale he ceased his 'card carrying' political activities while remaining a left-wing activist for the rest of his life. The move to Armidale was a bit of an aberration for the family as Armidale was a country town in the 1950s even though it had a university, teachers' college and a couple of expensive private schools. Daphne hated Armidale from the very beginning and she felt isolated. There was no opportunity to work and she was not a 'ladies auxiliary' type. She did run children's folkdance lessons which she had started in Heathcote but not being able to drive was a disadvantage now that there was no convenient public transport as there had been in Canberra. Don would drive to the university on the other side of town each day and after work there was always a lively scene at a pub called Bruyn's Caledonian Hotel in the main street. Another popular hotel was Tattersalls but this was considered more suitable for the squattocracy. The pub life in Armidale in the 1950s meant many women and children spent evenings by themselves during the working week.

The house in Mann Street was on a double block so Don and Daphne tried to make use of the extra land. There were lots of fruit trees, a wood shed, garage for the car and motor bike (an old Indian), a cubby, chook pen and lawn, flowers and hedges at the front. A paddock at the back contained a wood pile and a neighbour used it for her horses. The chook pen was a failure as Don chopped the head off one chook and the rest died of old age. One particularly annoying chook, called Henrietta, would follow members of the family around and try to constantly attract attention. She particularly loved sitting in the peg basket if a person was hanging out the washing. The fruit trees were more successful as Daphne had a Fowlers Vacola bottling outfit and the pantry was always full of preserved fruit. We had preserved fruit and homemade ice-cream for dessert every night. Don also took to the fruit trees with enthusiasm. He had a book called, *Home wine making without failure* by an H.E. Bravery. In the preface Bravery wrote:

> Those with gardens and those within easy reach of wild fruits and flowers are lucky, for they need only four pounds of sugar and threepennyworth of yeast to turn out a gallon of wine almost

indistinguishable from commercial products costing fifteen shillings a bottle.

At weekends, as Bruyn's pub was only utilised on work nights, many a party at the Atkinson's involved imbibing peach, pear or apricot wines.

My brother, David, was born in Armidale in 1961. He was sick at birth and spent some time in the Armidale hospital. Daphne looked after him when he came home and we had a phone connected for the first time in case of emergencies. Dons' father, David, always said that my brother David only survived because of Daphne's devoted care. David was eventually sent to a hospital in Sydney and Daphne went to Sydney and stayed at Don's parent's place while he was being treated. David spent months of his first year in hospital. My grandfather, David, died in 1963 and Annie came to Armidale for some time. Professor Jack Somerville, Don's boss and a person he had great admiration for also died in 1963.

Don was beginning to think that Armidale had played a significant role in his life but it was possibly time to leave. He began to explore his options through the international communist organisations that were associated with the Australian Communist Party. He had decided to go overseas, he was still disgusted with the job rejections he had suffered because of his ASIO adverse rating and he had now worked with and socialised with people who had experience of the outside world. One close friend from Sydney had been to the Soviet Union and China as early as 1955. Don began to seriously study what was happening in the rest of the world. He was interested in the experiences of countries who were beginning to gain freedom from the colonial powers and he wanted to help such post-colonial societies. He explored a number of options and a possible destination became Ghana. Don studied the Ghanaian revolution and decided he admired Kwame Nkrumah and sympathised with his pan-African politics. He resolved he would join other left-wing scientists and engineers in West Africa at the end of 1964.

Don told everyone that he was going to Ghana for a period of two years, maybe longer. I think he hoped it would turn out well and we would stay permanently. The house in Armidale was sold. Six months before it was sold a family room had been added at the back. Daphne complained that they only fixed places up when they were leaving, not to live in themselves. The furniture was sold and Don's precious car, a Plymouth, nicknamed Jellyroll Morton, was sold to Uncle Vern. This car was big and had venetian blinds at the back. Vern drove us to the airport in Jellyroll and then took 'him' home. Jellyroll would not fit in his driveway. While leaving such precious belongings as Jellyroll behind Daphne and Don decided they had to take the family piano to Africa. This same piano would return to Australia when they came back to Adelaide. It would finally follow my family to Wollongong in 1988 where it was eventually lent to a local childcare centre as the centre had a choir attached. After I left Wollongong my older sister was to organise the piano to Sydney for her step children.

The family moved to Ghana in 1964, returning to Australia at the end of 1965 by which time Don had taken a position at Flinders University. At the time it was still part of the University of Adelaide but it would get its independence six months later. This move was a permanent one in that Adelaide became the Australian home base for the rest of his life. However, considerable time was spent in Nigeria. He took time off his Flinders work to go to Nigeria in 1970 for a year. Wary because of the Ghana experience he did not sell the Adelaide house and did not resign from his job. However, the Nigerian experience was a success and after the fate of the electric car project was sealed by the South Australian and Federal governments he resigned and took contract positions at Ahmadu Bello University from 1975 to 1983. Though Daphne and Don spent most of their time together it was during this time that my mother felt compelled to come back to Adelaide so my brother could complete his high school studies in Australia.

Across all the years spent in Adelaide Don retained his interest in political struggles in Australia. He had a long-term interest in Aboriginal rights issues and from 1966 he became heavily involved in the Gurindji fight for land rights. He was involved in social movements like the one against the Vietnam War and was active in the idea of liveable cities, which was a theme underscoring many of his activities. Even the electric car project was prompted by a desire to develop a small, inexpensive, city run-a-round family car that would not be a dangerous pollutant. Alternative energy became a driving interest and this motivated many of his activities in Nigeria. He was also influenced by the *Small is beautiful* movement[3] for a short time.

The *Small is beautiful* influence led to the setting up of a small electronics business in a studio in the backyard in Adelaide with the words "Small is Beautiful" over the door. He designed cheap amplifiers and at one stage made science kits for schools. I suspect these kits were conceptually excellent resources but packed in plain white boxes with xeroxed instruction booklets they may have missed out on the glamour that more commercial products could offer. He did sell science kits to the Education Department in Victoria in 1978. The exercises and experiments in the kits were staggered across the primary years. When my son, Morgan, was four Don gave him one of these kits and they started to work through the activities. One of the early exercises consisted of two dice and a little booklet. Every time Morgan threw the dice he would count the number and write it in the book. Seven was the magic number that came up most. Another exercise for the very young consisted of a torch globe with an active (red) and neutral (black) wire soldered onto it and a small battery. The light came on when the wires touched the top and bottom of the battery in the right order.

As a kindergarten teacher at the time I would put this globe exercise out on the science activity table at the centre where I was working. There were children who were fascinated and couldn't get enough of trying to trick the globe. They would sit for hours touching the globe with the wires, enjoying turning them around, trying both on the top or bottom, to make sure the globe and battery would only interact in one way. This was in contrast to a state-of-the art stem set for kindergartens at the time that had some felt board circuits. Admittedly the felt board set had more than one type of circuit but I never saw a child engage with the felt board as they did with the hands-on torch globe. Big or small initiatives Don was never going to make money. He wasn't profligate but he was no good with money. Although his enthusiasm for the *Small is beautiful* movement waned much of the work he did in his final years was directed at helping individuals.

Coming back to Australia in 1983 Don set himself up as a consultant and was involved in myriad activities. He moved across town because he wanted to put up an aerial that was higher than anything allowed in the suburb he was living in. He would use his short-wave radio system to start a magazine that would bring film reviews and political commentary to an Australian audience that was not well-served by the mainstream media. In 1985 a house came up for sale just down the street from where Daphne and Don were living. Don raced in and put $1000.00 deposit down and rang his mother, Annie and said she should sell her house straight away. You could do such things in those days. That act gave her another comfortable 10 years before she needed to move to a low care institution. Annie was a strong woman, she had even visited Don for a few months while he was in Nigeria and she was in her 80s.

To the end Don was a life-long learner and a creative designer. Only four years before he died he enrolled at TAFE (Technical and Further Education) in a CAD (Computer Aided Design) course. He enjoyed the course but would go home for lunch on TAFE days as he could not cope with the conversations of his fellow students. One time when he felt his age.

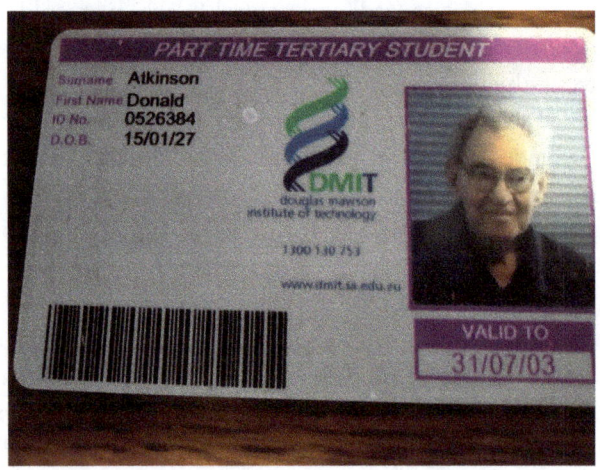

Figure 2.7 Student card of Don Atkinson for Douglas Mawson Institute of Technology 2003

Chapter 3 – Early influences

In this chapter I describe some of the influences that impacted on Don's life and choices he made. He was involved in many significant political, scientific and social events of the 20th century. Perhaps one of the earliest influences was being classified a security risk by ASIO as this was an incident that impacted on life choices and employment opportunities.

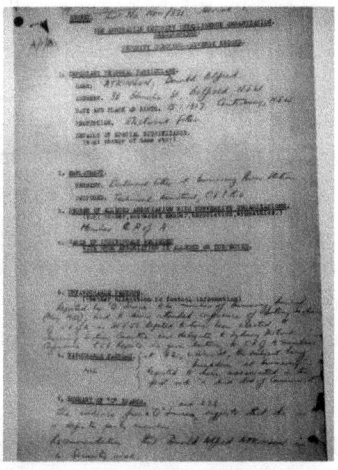

Figure 3.1 One of the entries in Don Atkinson's ASIO file determining his adverse security rating

The person who filled out the ASIO form above noted the decision to give Don an adverse security clearance and added there were nil "favourable factors" to mitigate this decision. This person did not know my father but got him right in that he would not be liable to change his spots. The information in the ASIO files is limited and I can't imagine it was very useful. Lack of technology meant most of the material seemed to consist of number plates of visitors, gossip from neighbours and spies at meetings. The meeting reports were mainly in the form of minutes, often finishing with a note to get the gestetner fixed. There were some comments in the files that reverberated. One person remarked that Don always greeted people with a "g'day matey". The informant thought this was affected and observed that it was probably Don's way of establishing his political ties to the working-class. Whatever the case years later my sister bumped into a friend of Don's and she was talking to him when his mobile phone rang. The ring tone was "g'day matey". He said he had put it on his phone as a reminder of his close friendship with Don. ASIO perhaps did Don a favour as his horizons were almost certainly broadened by the job rejections he faced in the 1950s. These denials led to him gaining a position at the University of New England which was a defining moment in his life. The university employed four staff members on meritocratic grounds who were all considered seditious. Russell Ward, one of the four, wrote of this event in a chapter in a book called "The New England Experience" and he named the four. The staff members employed at this time were himself, "Don Atkinson, a technician in Physics, George Pittendrigh for many years Warden of the Union and Eric Fry with whom I shared a tiny room in an old army hut below the Bool tennis courts".[1] The Vice-Chancellor at the time, Robert Madgewick, spoke of this act many years later as one of the proud moments of his life.

Russell Ward went on to spend 23 years in Armidale and in his speech on retiring from the university harked back to that moment.[2]

> When I came here 23 years ago I had already been kicked out of two tertiary teaching institutions because, as Sir Phillip Baxter, the Vice-Chancellor of the University of New South Wales at the time, informed the Council, my "character and reputation were such that [I] could never conceivably get a job in any university". Baxter admitted that he was acting on the scholarly advice of flat-footed, secret policemen who were quite unknown to me but not, probably, to him.
>
> These things were widely known in New England as in the rest of Australia; yet here was a university supposedly dominated by conservative rural politicians, knowingly appointing **four** reputedly seditious persons to its staff. I know from people who were members of the University Council at the time, that there was no attempt at dubious manoeuvres behind the arras. The academic selection committee made their recommendations on purely academic grounds.

The family's move to Armidale created new possibilities. After the move to Armidale Don's work gradually changed in complexity and opportunities for more creative work were presented. His activism as a left-wing reformer also found new boundaries to the extent that when he left Armidale it was to spread his wings on the world stage. Such a move meant his skills and imagination had become as important to him as his ideology and he had something practical to offer the world. He moved beyond loyalty to his communist ideals and developed a level of independent thought that provided a strong moral core to sustain future activities. Armidale was not the start of his growth and he did bring considerable experience on which to build during his years at the University of New England. Armidale was also not a place where he wanted to spend the best years of his life.

Don studied throughout his life and had an approach to living which made all his experiences valuable. He had enjoyed making things with his father when he was young. From his first position at Braybon Brothers he built on his love of machines and how things worked. He moved into the world of electrical engineering and this move gave him a distinct sense of the aesthetics of machinery along with a combination of idealism and a passion for tools. Daphne described his early interests:

> We always said Don was born with a 'cat's whisker'. His dad and he were into crystal sets of the 1920-30 period when he was very young. School did not impress him, I think it was all too slow and too narrow. He got himself an apprenticeship at Braybon Brothers in Sydney when he was fifteen and went to the Sydney Technical College, as it was then, after work for theory studies. He told me he saw an announcement for a lecture, which caught his interest and he attended on impulse. The lecturer stated he considered the future of mankind lay in Education and Electricity. Don didn't think he was much good at education so he chose electricity.

He loved images of coils, as in Tesla circuits and had huge admiration for Faraday. In his later life, when he started working with computers his home page always consisted of pictures of coils. He had originally set up his own company in Armidale called Atkinson and Associates but after he left his work at Ahmadu Bello University, in Nigeria, he set up a company he called Teslafarad. The name reflecting his two scientific heroes. The logo for Teslafarad was a Nigerian northern knot that was a symbol adopted in the 1950s as the country was gaining independence from Britain. It was said to represent the idea of unity in diversity.³ The logo was an indication of the continuity of his love of science and also incorporated his feelings for post-colonial Africa. He did not move from one enthusiasm to another but built on each experience across his life. Possibly why he managed to maintain energy and hope until the end.

It was during his time at Braybon Brothers that Don became active in politics and this involved both the union movement and the Communist Party. Sometimes they were combined. Don remembered that one of his first political acts was joining a protest march for day release for the training of apprentices. At the same time, he was becoming a part of a group of young radicals who would introduce him to aspects of life he had not encountered before. There were meetings, study groups, selling *Tribune,* the Communist Party of Australia (CPA) paper, previous to 1939 known as *The Workers' Weekly* and for the first time in his life lots of parties. When Don went to work at Bunnerong power station, after Braybon, the camaraderie was strong as there were many party members, or fellow travellers employed at the plant. It was also a union stronghold.

The CPA had been an illegal organisation at the beginning of the war but Don had been too young at the start of the war to have much awareness of these events. Now at Bunnerong in the early 1950s the CPA was beginning to face the challenges that McCarthyism had brought to America and it was feared the party might be declared an illegal organisation in Australia.⁴ The days of the Menzies communist dissolution bill created heightened feelings amongst the comrades that led to the forging of close lifelong friendships and some rather hysterical activities. In America communists were under attack⁵ and some gained particular following in Australia. Don followed the troubles of American communists like Steve Nelson closely. ⁶ Steve Nelson was a unionist, had fought in Spain and in the 1950s was sentenced to 20 years gaol for sedition. Charges were dropped after 6 years. Many in Australia were shocked when the Rosenbergs were executed in 1953.

This heightened atmosphere, coupled with the idea that the party in Australia might need to go underground led to some adventurous behaviour. The party had a shack at Terrey Hills, in the northern suburbs of Sydney. This shack was off an unmade track, referred to as Taronga Road, and hidden from sight. According to ASIO Don and friends would arrive on their motor bikes, spend a day or so on weekends and seemed to be preparing the shack as a safe house "when" the CPA became illegal. They disguised their identities and Don called himself Dr Atkinson from Paddington and received letters at the local post office addressed to same. His good friend 'Dr' Eric Parker also adopted a similar disguise. It is noted in the ASIO report that "discreet censorship of all incoming mail be carried out." Don told us he and Daphne lived at the Terrey Hills place for a while but if so I am not sure when. Mayo and I were born in the Royal North Shore Hospital but I can't find any other corroborating evidence. I know Don had a side car on one of his bikes. The idea of driving into the Sydney bush with Daphne in a side car clutching two babies is hard to contemplate. Though the fact that the older baby was called Mao is an indication of their political commitment at the time. As Australians in 1950 pronounced Mao as if it rhymed with the biscuit Sao it was easy for my sister to add a 'y' to her name. What could have been a constant embarrassment came to be considered an unusual name with most assuming it had an Irish origin.

The activities at Terrey Hills, given the circumstances were probably a form of bonding and helped build lifelong friendships, memory and trust. Certainly, the Parkers were important life friends. The fear of illegality and the measures put in place to be able to continue the good fight, if the Menzies dissolution bill had been successful, was long remembered. At my grandmother's funeral Don and a conservative cousin laughed about how she had hidden a type writer and other materials under her bed for him all those years ago. After 50 years they were still able to enjoy their youthful enthusiasms.

These were the days of the Sydney 'push' and although Don was young and too serious about his communism to be an integral part of the push he certainly enjoyed the discussions in the pubs. Sydney pub life was bigger than 'the push' and he also met legends like Lennie Lower,[7] a writer and journalist for whom he had an enormous appreciation, perhaps even love for the man and his words. Don hung around one of the bars in Sydney that Lower used to drink at and to this day the *Criterion* has a sign on the wall stating that Lennie Lower used to drink there. Don loved to tell Lennie Lower stories. Interested in the CPA Lennie Lower was given a faint reception by the party faithful who considered him unreliable because of his drinking but also probably more for his irreverent attitudes to people and things he considered pompous. Don used to tell how Lennie Lower would pawn his typewriter from the newspaper office to buy drinks and once even lost the ticket when he needed to redeem the typewriter. According to Don he was found crawling around the pub looking for something. When asked what he was looking for he said, "I'm too bloody proud to tell you but you can help me look." Don always liked a good story.

An opportunity to immerse himself in intellectual argument was one of the opportunities the left provided, developing lifetime friendships with like-minded people, an ever-increasing social circle that came from membership of a group and an expanding vision of his life and purpose were some of the benefits Don gained during his early days on the left. These benefits included a growing knowledge of Australian history and literature, engagement with music and his increasing interest in science as a way of life. Music had always been important to him. Don had grown up in a house with the ubiquitous piano but his main love became his trumpet and jazz. The association with the communists in Australia and jazz was a strong one.[8] Australia was a culturally isolated place between the two world wars of the 20th century and it was the communist youth group, the Eureka Youth League Group, and it's Melbourne leader, Harry Stein, who would promote jazz in Australia. In 1945 Harry Stein formed the Eureka Hot Jazz Society and organised a national jazz convention. This was exciting music, often derided by conservatives and viewed as decadent, it was urban, working-class music that came from Black America. Lots of boxes to tick for an Australian communist struggling against racism and fighting for a more egalitarian society. Eric Hobsbaum (1990) said in his book; *The jazz scene*:

> the crucial factor in the development of jazz, as of all American popular music, the factor which more than any other accounts for the unique American phenomenon of a vigorous and resistant folk-music in a rapidly expanding capitalist society, is that it was never

swamped by the cultural standards of the upper classes (p. 43).

One of the things that Don loved about jazz was improvisation. I have seen him stand up in amazement when a musician produced a particularly exciting improvisation of a piece and he was not even aware he was on his feet.

Figure 3.2 *Don Atkinson with trumpet (undated)*

Don's enthusiasm for jazz never died but he also entered the 1950s folk revival, led mainly by communists, with enthusiasm. Daphne, with her piano accordion, had long taught folk dancing so when the New Theatre[9] decided to produce an Australian musical, *Reedy River,* her skills were in demand. The New Theatre in Sydney is the oldest continuing theatre in Australia as it was established in 1932 as the *Sydney Workers' Art Club.* It was strongly supported by the CPA and the unions who would take block bookings for performances to ensure the economic survival of the theatre in the early days. These plays were highly political and sometimes were performed at factory gates, building sites, the wharves and once in a mine. *Reedy River*[10] was produced in 1953 after premiering in Melbourne earlier that year. The play had a run of nine months in Sydney and was performed around Australia. Don helped with the lighting for the Sydney production.

The names of those involved in the Sydney *Reedy River* production were very familiar as it was the *Heathcote Bushwackers* who provided the music for the show. Daphne and Don were still living in Heathcote at the time and were friends with the group. Like my parents all were in the CPA. Chris Kempster, who wrote the music to the Lawson poem, *Reedy River*, as well as having a part in the musical, was brought into the band through his membership in the Eureka Youth League. He remained a good friend with my parents through the years though parted ways with John Meredith when he, Chris, became interested in singing harmonies and John Meredith thought he was getting too musically complicated for folk music. Daphne and Don would later perform in the 1958 Armidale production of *Reedy River*. The LP made of the Armidale production labelled "Not for sale to the public" was still in the record collection when the family home in Adelaide was packed up.

Figure 3.4 Daphne Atkinson in Heathcote, third from right with piano accordion

One of the songs in *Reedy River* was the *Ballad of 1891*[11] about the shearer's strike of 1891 which has a prominent place in labour history in Australia. The music was by Donna Bridges (Doreen Jacobs) and the music is interesting in its own right. Donna Bridges wrote this music in the 1950s and her friend Helen Palmer wrote the words. They copyrighted the song as many who performed it, or published the song, thought the *Ballad of 1891* was traditional and written by 'anonymous.' Years later Donna's son would lead the Sydney Trade Union Choir and this song was a mainstay in the repertoire. In 1989 (reprinted 2008) a book was published by a labour historian, Stuart Svensen, called *The Shearer's War*. This book dispels some of the myths about the legendary strike of 1991. One issue is that the song starts with the line; "The price of wool was falling in 1891" but the price of wool did not fall until 1892. When the choir approached Donna Bridges for permission to rewrite the first lines she refused to consider the proposition as she and Helen Palmer had taken out the original copyright, her friend was long dead and she did not want to change it. Don laughed at this. He had known Doreen since they were both young and found the situation amusing. He said this was how history and myth get mixed and it is how history gets written.

There seemed to be endless clubs to belong to, lots of political activities and a huge group of comrades, some of whom were also best friends. Among the clubs was the Modern Writers' Club, the Sydney Realist Writers' group who espoused social realism and out of which the *Australasian Book Society* emerged. The American bombing of Nagasaki and Hiroshima at the end of WW11 had shocked the world so ban the bomb and peace movements became common. Some, like the Canberra Peace Group, referred to in ASIO files, that Daphne and Don were prominent in were probably CPA fronts. Daphne was the secretary of the Canberra Peace Group and Robin Gollan, the historian, organised monthly lectures and local radio broadcasts for the group. Ban the bomb, peace marches, support groups for countries struggling to emerge from the colonial yoke kept activists busy marching. Some of these clubs provided intellectual stimulation. There were lectures, study groups, exhibitions, music groups and a growing number of Australian writers. The *Australasian Book Society* produced 53 books from 1952 – 1989. Authors, poets, painters and ordinary punters like Don would meet in pubs and talk politics, literature and happenings around the world.

While there was plenty of friends and people with stimulating ideas there were obviously plenty of dark moments. The working-class lad with three young children who was locked out of the job market because of his ASIO rating would have suffered anxiety. Becoming aware of the problems of Stalinism and the Soviet Union whilst still wanting to be a radical and believe in a better world was difficult. The disappointment of seeing with his own eyes the inappropriate aid the Soviet Union offered to countries like the Republic of Ghana in post-colonial Africa made him rethink how he could try to fight for a more just and humanitarian world. In the case of Ghana, having to give up on that particular adventure would have been very depressing as it was the first time he had ventured so far from his western Sydney background. Later, at Flinders University when he was suspended for a month and 'sent to coventry' by his colleagues for supporting the student occupation of the registry he must have felt pretty devastated. Staying on the left but no longer enjoying the camaraderie of belonging to an organisation meant he had to take responsibility for his own efforts, sometimes with only the support of immediate family and friends. He was not a good CPA member as events in the real world were always more important than the party line itself and he seems to have stayed away from internal party politics. This latter impression is from personal observation and his ASIO files. When he was critical it was about real- world issues that could be addressed. There is an example of this practical approach in the ASIO files. The Canberra Peace Group had arranged to have weekly broadcasts on the Macquarie Broadcasting Network, station 2CA, and these broadcasts were titled: "Voices of the countryside". Don criticised the quality of the broadcasts on the grounds they were humourless, there was no personal touch and the delivery had no feeling and appeared to be read. There was discussion about how the talks could be made more accessible to a 2CA audience. Fewer ideas and repetition was suggested as the present talks were more "suitable for the ABC" (ASIO file 9/6/55).

Don gave up on the party after his Ghana experience. He did not make a fuss he just quietly left but still remained a friend of the left. It was a move more in sorrow than anything else and even during the anti-Vietnam war days he could see that the CPA no longer had a vibrant presence or much appeal with younger demonstrators. He would still approach his party friends to help raise awareness and money for the campaigns that he was involved with but he was no longer one of the faithful.

For those who had been Stalinists there was plenty to come to terms with. Some experienced a sense of shame made stronger during the cold war when anti Soviet sentiment developed, the core of the Russiaphobia we see today. The history of the CPA, *Reds: from origins to illegality*, by Stuart McIntyre, 1998, is an example of how it is difficult to generalise the experience of being in the CPA. *Reds* covers the period 1920 – 1940 from the first meeting to the second-world-war and most of the emphasis in the book seems to be on the party leadership, official policy and ideology. Descriptions of people are often unkind. Don read the book and did not say much. He would certainly have felt that he was one of the Sydney alcoholics criticised by McIntyre if the book hadn't finished about the time he was becoming a radical. He would have been in the next generation of Sydney drinkers in the party. Don was a drinker but it did not influence his energy and levels of activism. It might even have helped. He was often the life of the party and could be funny. As he put his bottles out to be recycled one Sunday evening he was heard to say to a neighbour, "Well there is one alcoholic who is not anonymous." I picked him up from hospital after a heart issue. On the way home Don asked me to stop at a bottle shop. He went sailing in telling the young shop assistant he had just had a heart attack, "My doctor says I must drink two reds a day, he didn't say if that was bottles or glasses". The poor young man was astounded. Daphne read the book, *Reds* and cried. She said, "he [McIntyre] makes us sound like such idiots." Don did not live to see the second volume of McIntyre's history.

What Don did gain from his party membership was a number of things. He acquired an international network that made it possible to get his first position in Africa, he developed his own personal ideology that never faltered and meant he could try to give reality to his own ideas and interests. Such growth led to his work in climate science and alternative technologies from the 1960s onwards, his interest in developing an electric car and his enduring efforts to support Aboriginal struggles.

Don's ideas about science started to develop during his apprenticeship.

He moved on to the heavily industrial working-class environment of Bunnerong Power Station after Braybon Brothers. While at Bunnerong and still a very young gung-ho communist he wrote an article for the *Communist Review* titled: "The decisive role of the working class in relation to Australian science."

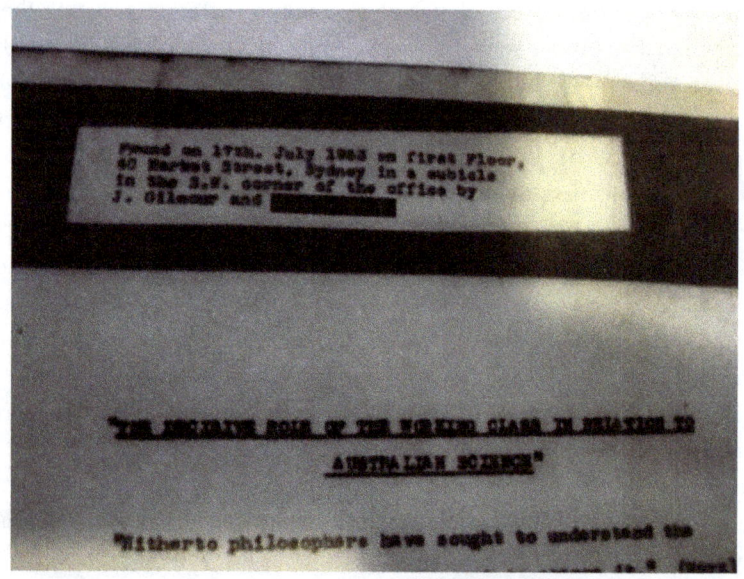

Figure 3.5 The decisive role of the working class in relation to Australian science

This paper was found in his ASIO file and the little square on the top of the paper (pictured) says: "Found on 17th, July 1953 on first floor, 40 Market Street, Sydney in a cubicle in the S.W. corner of the office by J. Gilmour and (name redacted)". An accompanying letter from Don to the publisher indicates the article was written in 1951. It is worth quoting some of the content as it is an example of how far the journey that Don's belief in science would take him if this article is viewed as an early expression of his ideas about the scientist and society. He started with three quotes; Marx, the eleventh thesis on Feuerebach, Humphry Davy on the creative powers of science and Engels at Marx' graveside making a statement on the nature of science. After this came the expected adulation of the Soviet Union.

> The Soviet Union is transforming nature. Flames of communism …
> are plans for peace on a scale hitherto unprecedented in history. In
> all fields soviet industry has made gigantic steps since World War II.

He then attacked America and warned Australia.

> As the Soviet Union and the People's Democracies attentively
> nurture scientific achievement Imperialist America destroys creative
> science … Cartel America replaces science with a military technique.
> Whatever Australian scientists may think of the quality of much of
> American scientific work, they must surely look across the Pacific if
> they wish to know the shape of things to come.

He went on to comment on the war in Korea and American scientists turning away from atomic research because of the warlike state of the US. He said state interference in Australia was stopping organisations like CSIRO from flourishing. He decried the money the Australian government was spending on "projects of death" like Woomera and jet aircraft while Australia needed the Lugarno power plant, and basic scientific analysis of soil depth and water bacteria on the Clarence River. The article then went into an argument on the responsibility of the scientist to help build a better world.

> The scientist can no longer stand aside. Decisions must be made.
> With Menzies – that way lies death and destruction; or with the
> forces of progress, in alliance with the labour movement – this way
> lies the future.

The paper finished on a rallying cry to the working class to help science out of its impasse. This paper was a measure of where Don the engineer was as a young man. As he worked and studied his ideas became increasingly sophisticated but the idea of the scientist's relationship and debt to society was a foundational one throughout his adult life. All his life he retained a belief in the potential of Australian science. He wanted to write a study of Australian advances in electronics in the 1930s and 1940s and had collected copious amounts of material that were still in his workshop when he died.

He was always thrilled when he came across something made in Australia. I can still remember an early washing machine in our house. The machine was a Lightburn, huge and resembled a cement mixer and it had the spin part at the front. The Lightburn factory was in Adelaide, Harold Lightburn had a progressive vision about building an inclusive workforce and designing and building inexpensive and reliable goods for the Australian market in the post-war years. A possible link can be drawn here between ideas Don developed for his electric car project at Flinders University and a small car, the Zeta, Lightburn produced in the late 1950s. The Zeta had a motorcycle engine, fibre glass body and was designed as an affordable city car. When Don became involved in electric car design in the early 1970s his aim also was to produce a small, affordable car, in his case though, with a clean source of energy. Lightburn had not got as far as pollution but there were similarities in the underlying aim for the two cars. In 2016 the ABC Drive show asked people to nominate Australia's biggest lemon. The poor little Zeta was nominated as the ultimate Lemon of a car by motoring journalist and historian Pedr Davis. He was a bit rude about the car and wrote:

> Some 363 Zetas were built. Awful though the concept was, it did have one good point. The owner could take out the front seats and clip them on the roof, which doubled as an observation deck. The idea was to watch sporting events at rooftop level, but most owners found it a convenient place to sit and wait until the NRMA van arrived.

A 'made in Australia' story that gave Don pleasure in his last days was an electric recliner chair. He had become increasingly weak and needed a chair that he could operate with a switch. A local company was selected from the phone book and Daphne and I went to order the chair. When I returned to Adelaide two weeks later the chair had been delivered and Don was thrilled with it. Hearing he was ill the factory sent a person to measure him up for the size of the chair. They made and delivered it quickly and bonus, it had an Australian motor. Not so good was that Don had chosen a bilious yellow colour and it had the most complicated and confusing controller ever seen.

Don became a good design engineer in his own right. During his university years he worked at New England and Flinders Universities in Australia, Legon University in Ghana and Ahmadu Bello University in Nigeria. His interests turned to the electric car, battery research, wind and solar energy. His commitment to science was supported by the work of scientists like Peter Mason.[12] Professor Mason was a contemporary who arrived in Australia in 1962. Mason was humanitarian, supported nuclear disarmament, was against the Vietnam war and believed in the advancement of science. In this capacity he developed undergraduate courses that combined social science, humanities and philosophy and emphasised the social responsibility of science. Don also established a Science and Society program which ran at Flinders University. Don's early enthusiasm for the Soviet Union was replaced by admiration for scholars and activists like Peter Mason. Peter Mason's broadcasts on the ABC *Science Show* were challenging and high quality. Don got such pleasure out of these broadcasts that he had a tape of the final lecture that Professor Mason gave on the radio and listened to it often enough that I think he knew it by heart. If you expressed an interest in the lecture a copy of the tape would be posted to you.

Don, the scientist, always wanted a practical side to his activities, he wanted to build things and this flavoured the choices he made during his life and the campaigns he participated in. One practical example is a project Don was involved with that concerned Cuba. The sanctions the Americans have exercised against Cuba are possibly the longest in world history. Some are historic, dating back to 1961 but more sanctions have been applied across the years with the Trade Sanctions Reform and Export Enhancement Act as recently as 2000. Don was happily handing around Cuban cigars at a Christmas gathering in Adelaide in the 1970s and someone asked where they had come from. He and a colleague, a vet scientist, had been involved in helping the National Poultry Union of Cuba build up gene banks for the poultry sector to establish breeding lines for different purposes. Eggs and poultry are a valuable source of protein and have played a major role in the nutritional well-being of Cubans since the revolution. Each year, near Christmas, Don would receive a large box of good quality Cuban cigars sent by his friends in Cuba.

Just as Don's scientific career grew from his early days in the CPA and union movement so too did his commitment to the Aboriginal struggle for human rights and land rights. The fight for Aboriginal justice was one that the unions and communists had long been part of. Many Aboriginal leaders worked with these leftists. Don maintained a strong interest and loyalty to this cause but the tenor of his engagement changed over the years. He became more confident in what he could usefully offer. After Armidale he was no longer a card-carrying member of the CPA although still very much of the left. Don was sensitive to being non-Indigenous, needing to acknowledge this while still participating in the fight for justice. As the years wore on he saw many people become despairing, some angry and there were Aboriginal people who did not want to work with whites or communists. There were Aboriginal people who preferred not to have communists as part of the struggle because they felt that anti-communist governments would be less likely to legislate in their favour. By the time Don became a participant in the fight for Gurindji land rights he was able to focus on the main issue, wait to be accepted and then involve as many friends as he could in promoting the cause and raising funds for the Gurindji cattle station.

Don became a radical for life and the form his radical activities took and the role his science played in this was a direct result of his experience. The early influences of his apprenticeship, meeting with committed unionists, his membership of the CPA all helped. Obviously, he had a personal proclivity to live an adventurous and exciting life and also a life of service. He rejected religion and a lot of the teachings of his parents by the time he was 15. At the same time, he always maintained a close relationship with his parents and remained a filial son, especially in the last decade of his mother's life. His strong belief in people, a faith in the potential of human beings was a driving force in his relationships.

Having said this there were sublime moments that are worth remembering. It was at a Christmas party in Adelaide in the early 1980s. Standing near a fireplace, clutching a drink was an old lady chatting to a young man. A few of us were close enough to hear her say, "and I said to Lenin". We were in the presence of history. The speaker was Marge Pollitt who, with husband Harry, had been a founding member of the Communist Party of Great Britain.

Chapter 4 Armidale

The family moved to Armidale in 1957. Although Don was one of four 'seditious' thinkers appointed at this time he had appropriate qualifications and experience to make him a strong candidate for the position of Laboratory and Workshop Manager in the Physics Department at the University of New England (UNE). There was no indication that his employment was not meritocratic. The qualifications required were a degree or diploma and a knowledge of instrument making. As Don had three trade certificates and a BSc he was qualified for the position. He always said that studying during the war had given him an advantage. When a shortage of materials occurred, he would need to be able to substitute and this gave him important design capabilities. Duties at UNE were outlined in his letter of appointment and included "supervision of Laboratories and the Workshop, maintenance of equipment, keeping of stores, ordering of supplies, and he will be required to construct and repair electronic equipment."

The registrar of the university was welcoming and arranged for Don and the Professor of Physics in Armidale, Jack Somerville, to meet in Canberra to discuss the move to New England and discuss plans for the department. The family moving costs would be paid by the university and Don was eligible for support under the university housing scheme. It sounded similar to arrangements today as he had to stay at least two years or reimburse the university for assistance he had received. By the time the family moved to Armidale Don had met his Professor, Jack Somerville, at least twice. They got on well. Dr Herbert Stock, son of family friends of my parents, who was in Armidale at the time, said that "everyone loved Jack". Jack Somerville had been one of the original academic staff at Armidale, having been appointed as a senior lecturer in Maths and Physics in 1938. He then moved to the University of Sydney and on the completion of his doctorate he returned to Armidale as Professor of Physics in 1953. He was unusual in that he had two undergraduate degrees, one in science and the other an arts degree. The surviving letters from Jack Somerville indicate a man who cared about the practicalities of life as well as a focus on his work. His letters give advice on moving, where to store furniture while looking for a place to live and also mentions work matters like the need to order a valve-tester.[1]

Figure 4.1. Professor Jack Somerville centre

Jack Somerville was an important mentor for Don. Reading descriptions of research activities in the research section of the *Science Journal of New England,* the magazine of the Science Society of UNE, Don was coming to an active department. In 1955 there were four projects being undertaken in the physics department. Jack Somerville was the lead researcher in two and was working in conjunction with the Electrical Research Board. This funding continued in the following year. In 1956 Sid Haydon, from physics, became the president of the Science Society and the secretary reported the society was looking forward to "renewed vigour" under the "enthusiastic leadership" of Dr Haydon. In this year Don's friend Kurt Landecker, from Sydney University, was appointed as a senior lecturer to the department. Research projects were divided into four major areas with many complementary studies being conducted within the research frame established. For example, 'Problems of electrical conduction in gases' were divided amongst the staff to experiment with arcs, electron multiplication at high pressures and electron multiplication at low pressures. The impression is of a committed team of researchers, working together across connected areas within their own areas of interest and expertise. This was the atmosphere that Don would come into in 1957. A work place where he already had friends and acquaintances and a work atmosphere that reflected the excitement of science in post-war Australia even in a cold war environment. A family friend who was a postgraduate in the physics department described it as "sound rather than distinguished".

Jack Somerville managed to invite trust and respect and I think the culture at UNE helped Don develop his ideas about engineers and technicians as crafts people and their role in the scientific process. An explanation by the Professor of Chemistry at UNE at the time, Robyn Stokes, reflects Don's growing awareness of the significance of the engineers. The following is an extract from an in-depth interview Professor Stokes gave for the series *Conversations with Australian Scientists* in 2009.[1]

> *The unique feature about Armidale and the chemistry department at UNE was the access to excellent electronic and technical staff.*
> I mentioned earlier my impressions about the importance of the craftsmen and technicians in keeping things going and making things. We were very fortunate in Armidale. We had a superb mechanical technician named Colin Tuxford. He was a fitter and turner, but also for very fine work he was unequalled. He is now unfortunately dead. But he was really out of this world in his ability to just take your rough sketch of an idea and produce very quickly a perfectly working piece of apparatus.
> As for glass-blowing, the first glass blower we had was John Clack, who was quite good; but Lloyd Hodges, who is still alive and still doing work for the university in glass blowing, could make almost anything out of glass. He was just so skilful it was really impressive. In making those calorimeters, for instance, he could take these little stainless steel paddles, which Colin Tuxford had made and seal them up inside a glass vessel without melting or scorching any of the metal. He was really quite exceptional, and he was one of the people who made the kind of work we did with the calorimeters possible. We just could not have done it without them.

Don also would wax euphoric over the work of those with exceptional skills in making things. In Adelaide, at Flinders University, he also worked with a glass blower who was outstanding, Roy Parrott. It is worth noting that Roy had talent as a glassblower and was also an activist. He was one of the supporters of the Gurindji land rights struggle and was also part of the Scientific Glassblowers Society of Australia. Roy served as a secretary for the society, was an industry specialist for the development of government training packages and although no longer practicing he was the International Liaison Officer for the society until 2003.

It was in Armidale that Don had the opportunity to settle into working with a diversity of scientists on a long-term basis. He could explore his own strengths and gain the skills to organise work space and working arrangements to enhance research capacity. This came to the fore after the science block at UNE, the Belshaw building, burnt down in 1958. This was an incident that had widespread repercussions. One scholar lost the only copy of his doctoral thesis. Don left a whole album of photos in his files of the Belshaw building in 1957 and then after the fire in March 1958. He had not had much time to establish himself in the laboratories before the fire and he then carefully followed the building of the new physics block in 1961-62. In between the fire and the new building laboratory work had to be co-ordinated in a series of small workshops.

Figure 4.2. The old Belshaw building and the shell left by the fire

It is worth digressing here to consider the excitement of the fire. When the fire broke out it must have been announced on the local radio. Our family did not have a phone until 1961 and lived on the side of

Figure 4.3. After the fire. Workshop 1960

Figure 4.4. New workshop 1962. Don always thought workshops should have polished parquet floors

Armidale away from the university. When Don found out his physics laboratory was on fire he decided to go to the university. He took my sister Mayo and me. We watched the building along with half the staff from the university and their families. My memory is dim but the photos on the net of this large building glowing from the inside is what I think I remember. Others had specific memories. Professor Stokes, whose chemistry building was next to the Belshaw Building, recalled the fire.[1]

> In February 1958, I got up in the morning and looked out towards the university and saw a great plume of smoke rising up and realised it was right on the site of my new building. So we rushed out in the car to see what was going on and found this old building, called the Belshaw building, was well alight and there was no hope of recovering anything.
>
> There were great explosions going on from exploding gas cylinders and a lot of general excitement. We were very concerned that the flames would spread to the closely adjacent new physical chemistry building, and we were racing around there with pieces of rubber tubing connected to the taps to spray down the walls to stop them from firing. One of our lecturers, Ray Stimson, got up in the eaves in the roof with some of his students and stopped the embers from getting in to set the place on fire; so that building came through it all right. But the destruction was pretty dreadful because nearly all the science departments had been completely wiped out and students had lost their honours theses and a lot of research work was lost. We also had the prospect of starting up a new term in a few weeks time.

The Belshaw building had been built in 1946 as there were many demobilised military personnel wanting to undertake university studies. The loss from the fire was enormous as laboratory equipment and research for physics, geology, zoology and botany were destroyed. The botany herbarium was gone and although many of the geology specimens survived the maps and survey documents explaining the collection were burnt. Others also had recollections. A blogspot has some anecdotes about the day.[3] I will cite a couple.

From Phil Emery. "When we arrived a fair amount of the building was alight and we were told to keep well clear (in hindsight we shouldn't have been allowed to go). I can recall seeing a couple of the firefighters throwing rocks at the windows around the top of the walls trying to break them so that their colleagues could get water into the building from above the fire and onto the spreading flames. No fancy extension ladders etc in those days for a small country fire brigade. Soon some of the kids who had gathered joined in the rock throwing and I remember thinking it must be okay if the firies were doing it."

From Paul Barratt. "There is one amusing anecdote to be told. In 1964-65 I worked in the ionospheric physics group led by Associate Professor Reg Smith. We had a piece of equipment that had been built in the Belshaw Block when Physics was there. It had never worked, and no-one had ever been able to track down the source of the problem. My older room-mate Bob Loch told me that on the day of the fire it had been thrown out a first floor window. From that day on, it worked perfectly. We put it down to a dry solder joint."

These two anecdotes were chosen as they represent different aspects of the experience and link to Armidale in different ways. There were many children watching the fire that day because this was a country town where major events tended to be shared and also it was the 1950s. Things were different. The 50s were another country. The second anecdote was included because it is connected to research being done by Reg Smith.

Don had a great enthusiasm for the parabola at the university and Reg Smith was involved in the construction of the parabola. Reg Smith was responsible for arranging a parabola from the CSIRO Division of Radio Physics from Potts Hill after the division moved its operations to the Parkes Radio Telescope. The parabola that Reg Smith obtained was small enough to be transported to Armidale and as family friend Herbert Stock says: "the road from Sydney was still rudimentary, narrow and dangerous with sections neglected after the war the Moonbi ranges were a horror strip until the 1980s". Herbert does remember that the 20m parabola built in Armidale was constructed in house so would have been a major project for the physics laboratory and thinks that the smaller

CSIRO parabola was probably used as a source for parts like gearboxes and motors of the steering mechanism "as these would be heavy (though small) and precision engineering using special materials that everyone would have been eager to avoid having to duplicate". The parabola was an important and romantic, piece of equipment for a physics department in those days. Don loved the parabola.

Figure 4.5. The Parabola at Armidale

Don's friend, Kurt Landecker, had come to Armidale from Sydney University. Their friendship stemmed from Don's Sydney medical school days and Dick Makinson, mentioned in chapter 2 was also part of the group.[7] Kurt was educated in Germany and came to Australia with degrees and a doctorate. He was also the first DSc (Science Doctorate) graduate at UNE. The DSc was a doctorate given in recognition of a body of work. He was appointed as a senior lecturer the year before Don arrived in Armidale. Kurt had been involved in the transmission and generation of radio pulses that could reflect off the moon. [4] The following story is told by William Blevins in one of the Interviews with Australian Scientists, series.[5] Professor Blevins would later move to Adelaide at much the same time as Don. The parabola played an important part in this research story. Dr Blevins tells that when Kurt had achieved results with his studies he tried to patent it but the Americans would not permit the patent for security reasons. They thought the research could have useful military implications. This was in 1959. The Americans persuaded the Australian government to take the same stance. Kurt's research could not be published and he could not take out a patent. It was Professor Jack Somerville who got the ban overturned and Kurt published a scientific paper with CSIRO in 1960 and took out his patent[6] in 1961.

Jack Somerville was greatly admired by both Don and Kurt. When Professor Somerville died Don wrote to Kurt, who was then in Geneva with the European Organisation of Nuclear Research, to suggest that Jack Somerville's name should be "memorialised in tangible form appropriate to the dignity of his life and work".[7] Kurt agreed and said he would do what he could.

In the letter he also mentioned Don's plans to relocate to Ghana and hoped they could catch up in Sydney before Don moved. Kurt commented that he needed to go into hospital for a minor operation. "Unfortunately, the shock of Jack's death must have affected me in some sort of a way." He said he had developed a back problem. Like Kurt Don was shocked by Jack Somerville's death at the age of 52. He always kept a portrait of him on his office or workshop wall, for the rest of his working life. I always thought it was Professor Somerville's death that had persuaded him to go to Ghana but the dates are too close. He could not have organised an overseas position in such a short time so his motivation for leaving Armidale is not clearly known.

The idea of a suitable memorial for Jack Somerville was also something Don took up with his friend Russell Ward who was still in Armidale. Russell wrote to him in June 1965:

> I passed onto Bert Madgwick (the VC) your thoughts about a J.M. Somerville Chair of Physics or some other suitable form of memorial for old Jack. Don't think it will do much good. Bert seems to have the idea that something like a bronze tablet let into the wall inside the Physics building somewhere would be the kind of thing Jack would have liked most. He was pretty close to Jack and possibly he may be right.

This first part of the chapter has focused on UNE and the university had an influential impact on Don's positioning of himself in the world of physics and university life. He was also involved in many other activities at this time, both recreational and political. One anecdote concerns the time when he decided to make a go-kart with frictionless wheels. The university used to sponsor an annual go-kart race and Don decided to make a kart. The rules were there had to be two on the kart so the boy next door was asked to accompany me on the go-kart. The kart was finally finished just before we had to go to the races so it didn't get a trial run. Don had built a kart with smooth metal rims and no tyres. He had some idea about what a frictionless wheel could achieve. Well we were almost shaken to pieces and the go-kart hardly moved forward on the steep incline where the races were held. One of Don's ideas that didn't fly.

Fresh from their theatre experiences in Sydney with *Reedy River* (chapter 3) Daphne and Don got involved in the Armidale production of *Reedy River* plus another Dick Diamond bush play based around Australian songs called *The Coolibah Tree*. Unfortunately, the souvenir program in the files, which was sold for one shilling, is undated. This play was presented by the Armidale Theatre Club. Don was in the production credits for the lighting. He was welcomed to the Armidale Theatre Club in October 1957. The club had about 250 members so amateur theatrics were popular in the town. Don joined the club as their new electrician and was described as a "valuable acquisition" in the club bulletin. Unless the club changed its name there seems to have been two dramatic societies performing in Armidale at the same time. The Armidale Theatre Club and the New England University Dramatic Society. Don did the lighting for both groups according to the programs and the plays all used Armidale Town Hall as the venue. Plays included Emlyn Williams, "A murder has been arranged", Lillian Hellman, *The little foxes*, Thornton Wilder, *Our town* and J.B. Priestly *Try it again*. So, we have a melodramatic thriller, a narrative of hate and greed, a timeless story of love, life and death and Priestley's approach to playing with time and the idea that the circle of life can be mended. I am reminded of the television advertisement for *Midsummer Murders* when the young constable says; "What more do you want?" A typical list for amateur theatrics in the 1950s.

An unusual thing that Don and Daphne embarked upon was an

interest in longevity and well-being. As true children of the age the cupboard in the bathroom would have put modern chemist shops to shame. There was a pill for everything. Some were probably useful. Us four children were given weekly fluoride pills. Don had read a book by/ or about a Rumanian physician called Ana Aslan[8] and he was interested in her work on gerontology and geriatrics. She had experimented with the effect that procaine could have on arthritis. Procaine is a local anaesthetic that was used in dental procedures. Dr Aslan ran a clinic in Rumania that became world famous among the rich as the drug was labelled a fountain of youth drug. Daphne and Don were not rich, certainly never went to a private clinic or had travelled overseas at this time but they managed to organise a supply of the drug from West Germany. It was called KH3 and they arranged to import it into Australia. The drugs came in plastic boxes. They were a creamy white colour with big red letters on top, KH3. The boxes were unusual at the time because there was not much plastic packaging about. That they were able to contact suppliers may have been through contacts in the communist party. The importation of such things into the country is probably also a sign of the times. It was eventually banned in America in 1982 but I cannot find if a similar action was taken here in Australia. There seems to be an anti-wrinkle cream called Gerovital H3 available through Amazon but I suspect this is a far cry from the tablets Daphne and Don were taking. By the time they had been overseas to Ghana and then moved to Adelaide such things were no longer of interest to them and they were becoming more attracted to ideas of sustainability and conservation.

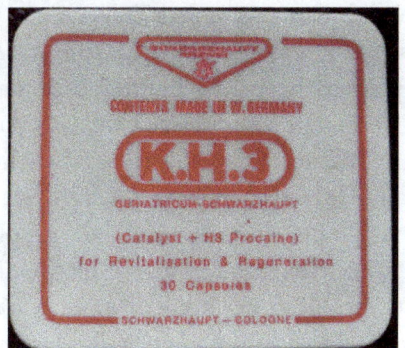

Figure 4.6. KH3 container

Don was still in the Communist Party during his time in Armidale, though numbers were small on the tablelands and monthly meetings were held in Tamworth. Don would go to these meetings and take one of us children with him for company on the drive. From the atmosphere of the meetings they were fairly dry exchanges of information. From a vantage point of sitting in a corner with a book to read I can vaguely remember usual reporting on *Tribune* sales and membership numbers and then a visitor would present on an issue of interest and answer questions. Visitors would be from overseas, other states, unions and the like. As well as party meetings in Tamworth the *Australasian Book Society* (ABS) would organise for the most recent authors to visit the capital cities and larger country areas, like Armidale. Don seemed to be the main organiser of these meetings and the authors often stayed at our house. I am not sure why this was the case but Don always enjoyed being mine host and he would certainly have been willing to volunteer. The social scene in Armidale was similar to that in Canberra where many meetings and parties were held at Daphne and Don's place.

Some of the authors I remember more than others. The evening with Ron Tullipan[9] was a successful one. His 1962 book *March into morning* had won the Mary Gilmore Award and he was already a recognised writer and a committee member of the Fellowship of Australian Writers. Although writers like Patrick White were becoming popular there were still plenty who would come and discuss a social-realist book like *March into morning*. Tullipan's theme was developed around the raising of consciousness through his main character Arthur Chapman, 'Chappie'. There are aspects of Chappie's life that resembled Tullipan's in that Tullipan had been in a children's home and his first marriage was to a 14-year-old. In this book Chappie had been in a children's home and one of the characters is Mavis, the tragic child-wife. The ABS published four new Australian books in 1962 so it was a busy year. I think Ron Tullipan may have been shy as I remember he was very quiet but then he was surrounded by people who knew each other and had plenty of opinions.

Another author who was popular was John Manifold[10] who came through Armidale to promote his book *Who wrote the ballads: Notes on Australian Folksong* in 1964. This was one of the last evenings that Don and Daphne entertained ABS authors in Armidale as it was the year the family left. John Manifold was different from other members of the Realist writers' group. He was born in Toorak, went to Geelong Grammar for a while and then went to Cambridge to study modern languages. His was a background of privilege and his life experience was in stark contrast to someone like Ron Tullipan who listed his occupations as labourer, writer and soldier. Ron had also had to take to the road with his swag during the depression. Different lives but shared values. Manifold joined the Communist Party of Great Britain while he was at Cambridge. This gave focus to his music collecting, his poetry and his interest in folklore. John Manifold was a performer and the night he presented his book to the group in Armidale was magic. He talked, sang, encouraged others to join in and it was a long, noisy night.

Books had pride of place in the house and as well as the ABS books and the English left book club books a travelling salesman talked Don into buying the encyclopedia *Britannica*. This was a big sale and the encyclopedia had to be paid off in instalments. It came with its own bookcase which fitted the original volumes neatly but when the year books arrived they had to be housed elsewhere. Pidgeon's Bookshop in Beardy Street was a popular haunt. A favourite activity was every Saturday morning the family went to town to select books at the local library to read for the coming week. Love of reading extended to mealtimes. We always sat around the table to eat together but a family preference was 'book-meals'. Everyone would bring a book to the table and we would read as we shared our meal. Only David was too young for this pastime but as a baby he was fed earlier. The other book occurrence was a man called, Bluey, he had red hair and would pass through Armidale and stay every so often. He, like the encyclopedia chap, was a travelling book salesman but his books were from the Moscow Foreign Languages Publishing House. Hard covered, beautifully illustrated these books were presumably issued through the communist party bookshop. I still have a copy of a book of folktales by P. Bahov, illustrated by O. Korovin and translated by Eve Manning called *The Malachite casket: Tales from the Urals*. The original price was 15 shillings but it was marked down to 9/6. Still a hefty price for the time and still a beautiful book. It was only in Armidale that I remember Bluey visiting so maybe he travelled around country towns and customers in the cities would go to the local party bookshop.

He only sold Soviet publications, the Chinese literature was becoming available through designated bookshops but was not yet available in country areas.

The other family literary activity was the radio. Don was an avid listener all his life and later in life would leave the radio on all night. The radio was an important link to the outside world. He listened to international broadcasts on this short wave set up and later he even tried to set up his own magazine through material he gained from his shortwave set up. Listening to radio all night is a bit of a family trait. Daphne used to complain when Don had the radio on all night but after he died she would leave the radio on. My sister Margaret and brother David also have the radio on during the night. They must find the sound soothing. In Armidale my sisters and I were avid Argonaut fans. Mayo and I joined the club but the names I remember for our ships are not listed on the web so memory fails again. I think even Daphne liked listening to the Argonauts. The other listening activity we did, as a family, was to listen to the Sunday night play. This was a whole of family activity, except for the baby and was something that was very much part of the family routine.

Don and Daphne kept contact with left-wing friends from Heathcote, Sydney and Canberra. They remained in the Communist Party in Armidale and were also in the Australia-China Society (ACS) (later the Australia-China friendship Association). There is a 'Greetings' card from Margaret Parker in their letter collection. The Parker family were an important part of Don's political journey. My younger sister was named after Margaret Parker. The stark word 'Greetings' on the card was Margaret's way of making a statement about Christmas. The card was printed in Shanghai for the Australia-China Society and portrays Picasso's peace dove in a white paper cut out on a green background. The printed words in the card are a verse from Beethoven's *Ode to Joy*, as sung by Paul Robeson. It is the verse that starts, "Build the road of peace before us". Don and Daphne's friend, Cecil English (Cess), was the president and national-secretary of the Australia-China society at the time. Cess was a friend of Don's in the Sydney University days. He was a medical doctor and also part of the Heathcote political and social scene. Daphne, Don and Cess enjoyed camping, bushwalking and were part of the folk revival. An example of Cess's involvement in the folk movement is told in an anecdote where he and John Meredith (of Bushwackers and musicology fame) were collecting folk music in London. They discovered an Australian/Irish folk song (Dennis O'Riley) and brought it back to Australia where it became part of the repertoire of Australian troubadour Edgar Waters. Edgar Waters subsequently took the song back to England and taught it to English folk singers.[11]

Cess went to a Youth Festival in Finland in 1955 and from there he was invited to go to China. Such an opportunity was extremely rare. There were 29 people in the Australian delegation in Finland and only 5 decided to go to China. It is worth remembering this was 1955 and travelling was less smooth than today. Cess sent a letter about his travels back from England where he was working in a hospital in Middlesex to restore his bank balance after his travels. He described this first trip to China.[12] An important contact for Cess was the New Zealander, Rewi Alley,[13] who was also in Finland and went back to China with the group. Cess would later work with Rewi Alley in China for a while. The group from Finland caught the train from Helsinki to Leningrad where Cess was able to visit hospitals, a blood bank and Pavlov's laboratory. From Leningrad he caught the train to Minsk, which he said was in a bad state because of the war and then the group flew to Moscow. After this it was the trans-Siberian. He said in his letter to Don: "You'd like the Siberians, rough, tough, drunken, untidy lot of bastards – just like Australians!" From Moscow to Peking took 36 hours. He found Peking hot, scrupulously clean and no flies. He thought the Soviets could learn something from the Chinese. He declared "here is the nation of the future." Cess was appreciative of how he thought the Chinese could blend long civilisation and tradition with progress. When he returned from his travels he visited Armidale and brought exotic presents from China. I still have mine, he gave me a hat and a ring. An embroidered hat which, according to google, is a Xinjiang Uighur dance hat. In an Australian country town in the 1950s such a hint of the outside world was wildly exciting.

Apart from the university Armidale had its charms. Wollomombi Falls was a favourite place to go walking and have a picnic, we would sometimes go and explore Hillgrove, which was pretty much a ghost town and Daphne had a cousin at Glen Innes. Don was active in the union and the union Christmas parties for families were fabulous. Often

Figure 4.7. Hat and ring brought back from China in the mid-1950s.

the children's presents were as good, or better than parents could afford. Don immersed himself at the university and in the pub life as well as remaining politically and socially active and keeping up with old friends and acquaintances. During his time in Armidale he saw at firsthand how first Australians in this country were treated. The politics of the Aboriginal struggle were very much on his mind. He was always distressed at racism and how it impacted lives. When the civil rights leader, Medgar Evers,[14] was assassinated in America in 1963 he was so angry he wrote to President Kennedy the same day. There is a rough draft of the letter in Don's papers. In his letter he recorded the time he first heard about the death on the ABC news and felt compelled to write about it. This letter to the President he wrote from the bottom of his heart and included statements like: "The human mind can hardly comprehend or measure this latest act of human slaughter." He references Richard Wright's biography, *Black Boy,* a book that is still sometimes controversial. Don admired the grandfather character in Wright's book and comments on the scene where Wright says the grandfather kept an old-fashioned gun by his bed. Don had his own interpretation of the old man's motive. "What a splendid and heart-breaking picture this forms of the militant old Negro whose hope in the liberation of his people is so absolute that neither time nor tribulation can shake it." The Evers murder has continued to shake America and Medgar Evers has appeared in protest songs, books and films over the years. A recent one was the documentary, "I am not your Negro", made in 2016. The film covers the deaths of Medgar Evers, Malcolm X and Martin Luther King Junior. Don would not have expected a reply from a 'Dear Mr President' letter but he felt moved to express some sort of protest.

Armidale was a class society. There was the squattocracy, the gowns at the university and then the town. I discuss Don and Daphne's distress about the Aboriginal reserve near east Armidale in a later chapter but there were many aspects of this side of Armidale that were omnipresent and there were a range of attitudes and ideological positions about the Aboriginal population. There was racism, paternalism and intolerance in various forms. The Armidale association for the assimilation of Aboriginal people (chapter 9) were well-meaning people whose patroness was the vice-chancellor's wife. In tune with the politics of the time this organisation believed assimilation was the best way to advance Aboriginal interests. Save the Children established a preschool in East Armidale in 1963 with a stated aim to assimilate the children. It was not until the 1970s that Save the Children started employing trained local staff, with knowledge of local culture and language, to work in these centres. Don and Daphne never quite fitted in. As communists they were committed to the ideal of rights for Aboriginal people, they were opposed to the idea of assimilation. They were sociable and enjoyed much of their time in the town but it was borrowed time. As an engineer and technician Don was not a 'real' academic. Their lives could have plodded on reasonably comfortably but I suspect this was not enough and was one of the underlying causes for the move to Ghana.

We left Armidale to move to Ghana at the end of 1964. Going through Don's papers it appears he started looking for an overseas placement in other parts of the world before he applied to go to Ghana. In 1963 he had approached the Indonesian government and received a charming note from the embassy regretting they could not assist but would note his interest with appreciation if the situation should change. He was determined to leave Armidale and it seems he wanted to also leave Australia. In Armidale he had worked with some good people, he had been reasonably energetic and had found the research exciting. In leaving there were two possible drivers. He still wanted to help change the world and the sojourn in Armidale had made him think that Australia was boring and had ingrained problems that were systemic. There was also the fact that although Australia was changing he had been rejected by most of the institutions where he could look for future work and he was determined to never go back. When he did return to Australia he took a job at Flinders University (it gained its independence from Adelaide University shortly after he joined the staff) as he said he wanted to go to a new institution that had not been part of the McCarthyism of the 1950s.

Figure 4.8. Don standing by a travelling wave oscillograph in 1960. It was made available to Professor Jack Somerville from the Atomic Weapons Research Establishment at Aldermaston (England) and could record events occurring in one thousandth of one millionth of a second. It was thought to be probably the only one of its kind in Australia at the time

Chapter 5 Ghana

The move to Ghana was a brave move for a family that had never left Australia. For Don the attraction was Kwame Nkrumah. Kwame Nkrumah was one of the most, or the most, important African leaders of the twentieth century. In 1999, in a BBC poll, he was voted "Africa's man of the millennium". [1] He was motivated by an ideological vision of radical socio-economic development for both Ghana and a United Africa with socialist ideals. Reading a study of Nkrumah's life[1] I can see that Don was impressed by many of his ideas before we went to Ghana and remained committed to lots of those ideas for the rest of his life, even though the move to Ghana was short lived (only the year 1965). There was a coup in February 1966. Two of the ideas that Nkrumah had that separated him from some of the other anti-imperialist African leaders of the 1960s and 1970s was the vision of a United Africa, so called Pan-Africanism and his belief that a one-party state could be democratic and look after its people. Pan-Africanism was a different stance than the one that would emerge from the African National Congress (ANC) in South Africa. Pan-Africanism as ascribed to Kwame Nkrumah was a belief that African society was a fusion of the traditional African way of life, with Euro-Christian and Islamic influences viewed through the lens of a dialectical materialist analysis. He believed Americans and others around the world of African descent were part of the struggle. Through his study and travels Nkrumah developed an extensive world-wide network of political, trade union and student activists. He wanted to build a nation that would hold together through its civil institutions and provide for all. Through this vision he hoped that different religions, languages and tribal membership would not be divisive forces that could be manipulated and exploited by those who would seek to contain African growth in the post-colonial era.

It was in London in 1945through to1947 that Nkrumah became a prominent actor in the anti-colonial Pan-African struggle through organising the West African National Secretariat (WANS). During this time, Nkrumah worked actively with many members of the Communist Party of Great Britain (CPGB). The international communist movement and trade unions gave him strong support. Don was familiar with George

Padmore's book, *How Britain rules Africa* [2] and this made him sympathetic to Nkrumah's ideas. Padmore was a radical journalist, born in Trinidad and was a leading Pan-Africanist. He was a strong influence on Kwame Nkrumah and died in Ghana in 1957. Don had read Nkrumah's 1957 autobiography[3] and participated in discussions on colonialism and Africa that were taking place in Australia. Some of this discussion took place in the Communist Party meetings he attended in Tamworth. There was also coverage in the newspapers and articles that appeared in the left-wing press of the time. A search through the Communist Party of Australia (CPA) paper, *Tribune,* indicates the CPA strongly supported countries like Ghana in the post-colonial era although there was little detailed reporting of events within specific countries. Some articles mentioned Ghana and other newly independent countries, but in the CPA the focus at the time was an adamant opposition to apartheid in South Africa and praise for what the Soviet Union was offering the "third" world. In the years while Don was in Armidale and preparing to go to Africa I found only four articles in the Australian left-wing press that specifically mentioned Ghana. One referred to Ghana as a place where a Soviet Science ship had visited (December, 21st, 1960). The CPA were also very Australian or English centric, so another article criticised the Australian prime minister, Menzies, for his enthusiasm for a Commonwealth that would include countries like South Africa and how insulting this must be for members like Ghana (March, 8th, 1961). However, as a long-time and active member of the CPA Don was able to join the CPGB. Through the CPGB he could access information and political documents on Africa. This was a period where Australia was still isolated in relation to activities around the world. It was because of his CPGB membership that Don was able to organise his application to go to Ghana to work at the Ghanaian University at Legon in Accra.

Education was important to Nkrumah. He was the prime minister of the country from 1957 and on independence became President of the Republic of Ghana from 1960 -1966. One of his greatest interests was education and he quickly tried to universalise nine years of schooling, eliminate school fees and improve the status and the teachings of the University of Ghana in Accra. The university had started as the University of the Gold Coast in 1948 and as a Commonwealth member had a special relationship with the University of London. By 1961 the University of Ghana was established as an independent establishment. The new university was built on Legon Hill. This was the environment Don was moving into. The following description is cited in Biten. [1]

> He wanted a socialist order in Ghana heading the African revolution to drive vestige of imperialism out of Africa and to liberate the colonially occupied portions of Africa. He wanted Legon to become the intellectual centre of the African revolution, of socialist Ghana, and of international study of Africa's past and future as one of the world's great continents and not as an appendage of western history, culture, economy and civilisation. The map (figure 5.1) below indicates the extent of university departments in 1965. The Balme library, in the middle overlooking open space and an ornamental pool, had 145,000 books. They were three short when Don left as he received an aerogram in 1967 saying he still had three books out on loan.

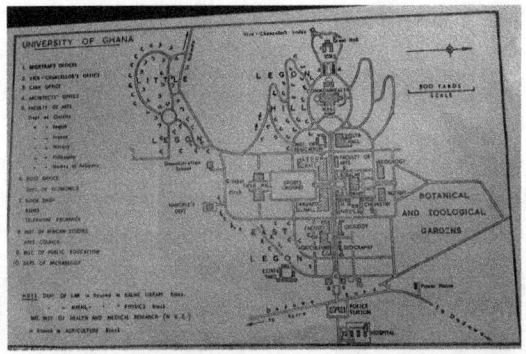

5.1 Map of the University of Ghana when Don worked there in 1965

There were a number of threats on Nkrumah's life. At the beginning of 1964, the year before Don arrived in Ghana, there was an assassination attempt on Nkrumah. There were difficulties within institutions and the Ghanaian government had issues filling positions within organisations like the university. Following the assassination incident in 1964 six academics from Legon university were deported as security risks. One of the deportees was especially influential and his work was one of the arguments used to justify the coup in 1966. This academic was Professor William Burnett Harvey who was Dean of the Faculty of Law at the university from 1962-1964. According to some accounts of the attack on Nkrumah Professor Harvey was accused of being a Central Intelligence Agent (CIA) agent. When the new law school at the university had been opened Nkrumah outlined his vision for the role of law in the Republic of Ghana. He saw the law as an instrument to help build socialism and a new more equitable nation. After leaving Ghana Professor Harvey published a book on the legal system of Ghana,[4] and expressed no sympathy for Nkrumah's vision. Harvey was considered an erudite scholar educated in the Anglo-American tradition. He appeared to have no love, or even an understanding, of a one-party state outside of a repressive dictatorship. He described Nkrumah as a dictator and this description was agreed to by many after the 1966 coup. The concept of a one-party state was the most controversial idea that Nkrumah had propagated and it found little support in the collective West. Don could sympathise with Nkrumah's argument and in later years would defend the idea and found interpretations of democracy, as practiced in the West, to be inadequate. These conflicts were indicative of issues facing Ghana and Nkrumah in 1964. We would arrive there in 1965 as the Nkrumah government was in its last year.

In terms of staff at the university there was one who Don was excited about the opportunity to work with. This person was the Professor of Physics, Alan Nun May, for some reason he was always known to the family as Nun May. Nun May gained notoriety when he passed nuclear secrets to the Soviet Union when he was working on the Manhattan Project during the war. Nun May had been at Cambridge at the same time as the spy Donald Mclean, one of the five Cambridge spies of notoriety. It was at Cambridge that Professor May became radicalised and joined the CPGB. After completing his PhD he moved into government research and university teaching. By 1943 he was working on an atomic reactor project with the Americans in Toronto. He worked on the Manhattan Project until 1945 and was arrested in 1946 when a Soviet agent he had passed information to defected. Nun May was sentenced to 10 years gaol in 1946 and released in 1952. After his release from gaol Nun May married Hilde Broda, a doctor. He was blacklisted at British universities and in 1961 Nkrumah invited him to Ghana as a research professor. Hilde was also able to work in Accra. Nun May and Hilde would remain in Ghana until 1978. When Don moved to Ghana Nun May was working in solid state physics, which fitted with Don's engineering past and Professor May had been tasked with establishing a science museum. The original Museum of Science and Technology opened its' doors in 1965. Such an initiative was something Don was very enthusiastic about. The museum was opened the year Don spent in Ghana so he was very much part of the project for the one year. The position at Legon University was suitable for Don's talents and interests as well as being enlivening in the sense that it gave Don an opportunity to feel that here was the opportunity to contribute to post-colonial Ghana.

This first trip overseas was exciting for the whole family. We flew to Singapore, Beirut and then to Ghana. In Singapore Don was met by a young doctor who was in the Communist Party. The young man took us shopping and then to a housing estate with a kitchen underneath where people could get take away food or eat on the premises. The containers for the food were grey pottery, shaped like a saucepan with a handle. They were very beautiful. Beirut was something again. The city was amazing. We had only ever been in hotels a couple of times in our lives. Don was excited in a bouncy way like a child. Driving from the airport he was exclaiming about things like what side of the road the cars were driving on. Beirut has always stayed in my mind. We were there for a couple of nights and spent the day walking around admiring the beautiful city. It is the only time in my life I have been in a place and was witness to something that was subsequently utterly destroyed.

Arriving in Ghana we stayed at a hotel and were then taken to the house that had been arranged. The university official was sorry but there were no houses available on the campus so we had one in the suburbs. A three- bedroom, brick house. There was a half-built servant's quarters at the back that was never finished. Daphne was relieved. She found the whole issue of servants very difficult. She had never been waited on in her life, believed in cleaning up after herself but also realised that people in Ghana, by 1965, were seriously poor so it would not have been right to sack the servant that had been organised. As it was he wanted to hire a younger man as well, a "house-boy" and Daphne said no. This could have been for financial reasons as well as the social awkwardness that she felt. I do not know what the university salary was like but we had come to Ghana with no reserves and there were six of us. Living in the suburbs meant Daphne was isolated again. She could not drive and we did meet some neighbours but they were generally working during the day. School was from 8 until 12 so we all came home for lunch.

Don would take us into the university quite often in the afternoon. We met the people he worked with. The Mays lived on the campus. They had a boy about Margaret's age and she would sometimes go to visit him. An accident happened one day when she was coming through the living room at the May's place. There was a heavy old-fashioned wood door and as Margaret followed the lad through the door he slammed it not realising she was just behind. The heavy door slamming sliced off the top of Margaret's finger. The doctors in the hospital were very concerned and grafted the top of her finger to her hand so they did not have to amputate to the next joint. Daphne, as a nurse, was impressed with the care given. The only other experience we had with the medical system was when my sister, Mayo, had appendicitis and malaria at the same time. The malaria was diagnosed but the doctors almost missed the appendix. Once they realised what was wrong treatment was fine.

The family is much more present in this chapter even though Don is the focus of the overall story. Being in an unfamiliar environment we were dependent on each other and we tended to do things together. This included making joint decisions about what we would do. An example of joint decision-making is that Don had a romantic idea that Mayo and I would go to a Ghanaian boarding school where we would meet local girls, learn about local music and dance and perhaps a bit of a local language. Mayo and I decided we were past such activities, we were interested in clothes and boys and said no firmly. He was disappointed and we went to the local international school.

I am not sure when Daphne and Don realised that it wasn't going to work. The year we were in Ghana was the last year of the Republic and Nkrumah's last year as President. It is difficult to pick through the relentless bad press that accompanies the dying days of a government. Don was working with people he liked but was critical of how little independence the university had and he was not happy with Nkrumah's leadership. When he decided to leave and take a position in Adelaide he sent a series of letters to a colleague already working at the University of Adelaide. The following quote reflects his dissatisfaction.

Figure 5.1 Mayo (on the right) and Berenice in school uniform outside our house in the suburbs of Accra

It is a pity that such a fine university (Legon) as this is being strangled by government interference but I can't see any hopes for a change while ever most things in the regime of Ghana centre round the whims of one man (Nkrumah). Last week the 'Great Man' himself sent me a note requesting a report on the Science Museum, so as he can decide on budget provisions for 1966. Presumably if he doesn't like a project it just dies, and I have literally seen that happen to two very fine research establishments in the last six months. ... Jack Somerville had an expression for those situations "It would make a cat laugh" and it really would.

Others reported similar disquiet. Russell Ward sent a letter from New England commenting on Don's enthusiasm for West Africa. He cited the experience of young PhD student he had worked with who had consequently gone to Ghana for two-and-a-half years.

I thought and think him a pretty well-balanced and very fair-minded old lefty. He says he loved the people and the country and of course approved the aims of the regime: but that after a year or two he became increasingly disturbed by the unexplained arrests of friends etc ... Hope he was unduly pessimistic about this.

There were few stories of satisfying projects and when Don socialised with colleagues it was more to complain about how things were going in the country. These conversations took place during frequent drinking sessions. There was endless gossip about the politics of Ghana and there was already a feeling that people were getting ready to jump ship. Some of this was understandable. Biten[1] cites the following story, told by the economist Dr Jonathan Frimpong-Ansah. Dr Frimpong-Ansah in 1965 was the deputy governor of the Bank of Ghana. The context was that the price of cocoa had fallen world-wide and the country had a large deficit.

> By 1965 it had become very desperate and I remember we decided to write a memorandum to Nkrumah to tell him the true state of affairs of the economy, I had written that the reserves were only 500,000 pounds. He looked at me and said "All! You didn't check your typing! You've left a few zeros!" I said "No Sir, there are no zeros left". This is 500,000 pounds - all we have in the banks overseas. And he sat back. And what he did then was that he went round the table and went to everyone who was seated there at the meeting and asked them: "Frimpong says we've 500,000 pounds. Is he right? Do you agree with him?" And everyone said: "Yes". That was the first time the whole cabinet acknowledged to the President that Ghana was bankrupt. When Nkrumah heard this he actually shed tears. He left us in the office in the Cabinet room for half an hour. He broke down completely when he knew that Ghana was in fact poor.

One of the observations that disquieted Don while we were in Ghana was the role the Soviet Union played in supporting the Republic. During 1957-1966 Ghana increased trade with the Soviet bloc. Ghana exported primary raw materials and imported manufactured goods. Don was extremely critical of the nature of the manufactured goods which consisted of items like tractors, transport equipment and agricultural machinery. Many recipients of these goods had neither the spare parts nor experience to keep them functioning. Don would get frustrated at seeing tractors and the like rusting away in plantations. Many projects were also ill-advised. Giant silos built by a Romanian contractor in the early 1960s were a disaster. It was found that "the combustion of cocoa kept in such silos in the tropical heat would burst them open".[1] Even the 600 students who had gone to the Soviet bloc to study suffered discrimination when they tried to return to Ghana after the coup.

Don had previously been critical of the devious face aid could take when he considered some of the awful tricks played on Australian Aborigines as they tried to establish co-operatives around the country. Now he was seeing it on an international scale. While an aid sceptic already he now saw it as a form of exploitation and imperialism. That it was the Soviet Union, that he had long supported, doing this increased the blow. It was this realisation that largely led to his indifference in rejoining the CPA when he returned to Australia. He found there was no stomach in the Australian left to even discuss such issues. Don's reaction to foreign aid hardened over the years. In 1974 he gave a lecture at Flinders University for the *Science and Society Symposium*. At the time he was the secretary for the National Committee of Engineers for Social Action (NCESA). He described the world as being divided into three; the rich imperialist states with America representing monopoly capital and the USSR representing state capitalist with socialist states in the second group and third group were the poor independent countries of Asia, Latin America and Africa. He denounced aid practices, especially those of the USA which was more likely to provide aid in the form of grants to advanced industrial societies while less than 50% of aid to under-developed countries was in the form of grants. In 1966, the year after we left Ghana, 44% of aid to under-developed countries was needed to finance past debt. Don pointed out that many poor countries were not much more than economic appendages of rich nations. He tried to end the time in Ghana on a positive note and he never lost his interest in wanting to see post-colonial Africa prosper. Even in 1974 when he had already been to Nigeria for a year, in 1971, he was still hopeful that there were many movements and struggles among workers and peasants in the poor countries that might prevail against the colonial powers.

There were aspects of the experience that Daphne and Don seized on eagerly. The markets, the market women, the craft and the food as well as many of the people they met meant they would go back to West Africa after four years in Adelaide and then continue to spend the best part of the mid-1970s to mid-1980s in West Africa as they moved between Australia and Nigeria.

Figure 5.2 An African tribal mask, probably from the Ivory Coast bought from one of the Hausa traders who would visit the markets

Figure 5.3 Ebony box with an Ashanti stool set in ivory

Wood carvings (examples above) were bought at the markets, Daphne and Don commissioned some pieces to bring back. The elephant coffee table (below) is an example and Daphne started to collect fabrics. In the mid-1960s items like the coffee table and many of the fabrics were still exotic in Australia. Food tastes expanded. Don developed a liking for semolina and okra, a taste not shared with the rest of the family. Back in Australia he would source his own okra for years and he was pleased when it finally appeared in the Adelaide market. Don also liked the West African shirts that the men wore. For the rest of his life he kept a supply of these and considered them to be the most comfortable form of dress.

A bonus was that books were very cheap compared to Australia and as reading was a major entertainment we would go to the university bookshop and pick out books to read for the week. The bookshop replaced the Armidale library. We were buying the books, not borrowing, so we tried to choose books that could be read by the rest of the family and also books that were worth keeping on the book case. All the family over the years have enjoyed these shared books even though Margaret and David were too young at the time. The shop was mainly dominated by the Penguin brand but the supply of classics and contemporary fiction was excellent. There was also an extensive collection of African writers.

Figure 5.4 Elephant coffee table commissioned in the Accra markets in 1965

Friends were important. Margaret and David were still in primary school and made friends with local children and families. Mayo and I, being at an international school mixed with a wide variety of others. There were drawbacks to this. My maths teacher was the loveliest young man and I am sure was brilliant at maths. He came from Cameroon, his English wasn't much good and my maths was already on life support. I always think that Ghana is where I finally lost my maths. This would lead to much painful studying as I struggled to pass public examinations later. One of my best friends was Aboshe. I wanted my ears pierced and Aboshe took me to see her grandmother who basically took a needle with a large eye, threaded about four pieces of cotton through, heated the needle in a candle flame, held a thin piece of cork against my ear lobe and pierced my ears by sewing a hole in them. I was so happy when I came home with cotton thread though my ear lobes. Poor Daphne had to find some sleeper ear-rings and fussed around with anti-septic cream while the ears healed.

Figure 5.5 David's class. David is the 4th from the right in the front row looking away from the camera

Don had friends at work. He socialised with many of the department who were made up of local scholars and many, like Nun May, who had been invited or volunteered, to help Africa's first post- colonial country. There were many young academics from around the world who had come to Ghana because of their political sympathies. Don soon had a drinking circle, a couple of young Irish scientists became particular friends. Daphne met a few people locally that lived around us. There were a mixture of people living nearby, many of them worked for embassies. Daphne and Don went to a couple of social evenings at the Australian High Commission that were held for Australians living and working in the country but quickly decided that they did not find these evenings very comfortable. The High Commission sent a form to be filled out so their details could be registered. The blank form was still in Don's files so presumably they did not pursue this contact. Given Don only spent a year in Ghana there were a significant number of invitations to cultural events and exhibitions from the Minister of Culture. These included exhibitions of children's books and toys in the GDR, Ghanaian pottery, Chinese ceramics as well as African art and dance.

Don and Daphne became close friends with a family from Melbourne, the McAdams, who lived about an hour north of Accra. We would visit on weekends. Ken McAdam was an education scholar who worked for the Institute of Education at the University of Ghana. Like Don Ken had arrived at his position through contacts in the CPGB. This was important because as the political situation declined Daphne and Don found it was comforting to be able to talk openly to a fellow Australian with similar politics about what was happening. The McAdams left Ghana the same year that we did and he took up a position at Monash University. He died in 1975 at the age of 55. One of his areas of study, as an educational psychologist, was on the nature of creativity and who is creative. Don would talk to Ken for hours.

We travelled around the country as a family and did as much sightseeing as possible. We visited the fishing village of Winneba. This was a major port during the time of the British slave trade and even before. Fort Winneba was one of the holding places for slaves while the trade was strong. The displays and leaflets available at the fort contained indictments of slavery in the strongest terms. This was important politically as well as historically as Nkrumah believed African-Americans provided the initial drive for the Pan-African movement. He considered Black-American politics and culture were strongly influenced by Africa. Nkrumah wanted to position the struggle for liberation facing countries like Ghana in a national and international context. He believed the history of slavery and the fight for Black rights in America and Ghana were intertwined. He tried to encourage a relationship and the government of Ghana had introduced initiatives like issuing special visas for the descendants of those who had been taken out of Africa. Nkrumah wanted justice for all Africans. I can still remember the visit to the museum at Fort Winneba. It was a graphic depiction of the slave trade. We also spent some time on the beach.

Figure 5.6 Margaret and David at Winneba

Another place in Ghana that I remember well was the Black Star Square. This is an enormous square built in the first four years of the Republic. In the middle is the Black Star Gate which has the five- pointed Black Star of Africa at the top. There is also the Independence Arch and a Liberation Day Monument. These are massive structures and the square itself is impressive and is the site of the National Independence Parade on the 6th March each year. In Don's files there are four admission cards for the 8th independence anniversary celebrations to be held in the square on Saturday March 6th 1965. The square itself was commissioned by Nkrumah and named after a famous shipping line, the Black Star Line, set up by the Universal Negro Improvement Association (UNIA) in 1919. The Black Star shipping line was established to promote commerce between Black communities around the world. It only lasted until 1922. Nkrumah would name Ghana's shipping line after the UNIA initiative and the Black Star was adopted as part of the Ghanaian flag. The star stands for freedom for all Africa.

When we were in Ghana there was the growing feeling of what was to come. Much of the media seemed to concentrate on Nkrumah's personality. He was accused of becoming a dictator. He was a private man who kept his family out of the press. He had married at 48 and his wife was a 22-year-old Egyptian woman. The scandal rags went to town. There was less coverage of the growing poverty and food shortages in the media than salacious stories about the man's private life and his young wife. There was malicious gossip and past events were confused with contemporary happenings. In the end it was sad. The following quote acknowledges the failure of Nkrumah's republic with regret. This statement is especially significant in that it was written at the time.[5]

> ... the failure of the socialist experiment in Ghana did not lie in the peculiarity of African circumstances, and still less in the psychology of a single man. It failed because the attempt to break with Ghana's colonial past was not made soon enough, and because when it was made, it was not complete enough.

Figure 5.7 Don and Mayo at the statue of the unknown soldier in Black Star Square. I suspect I might have taken the photo which is the reason the soldier is missing his head

The Ghana story for the family finished with Daphne, Mayo, Margaret, David and I going to London while Don stayed in Ghana to complete projects he had started. We went by boat to Liverpool and the life on the boat was another cultural challenge. Morning and afternoon teas, dressing for dinner, being waited on by young men was daunting. Daphne and a young Irish friend who was also going to the UK with her children spent anxious moments discussing things like how much they should tip the stewards who looked after the cabins. We caught the train from Liverpool to London and a taxi to the flat we had been able to borrow from English colleagues still in Ghana. It was late and dark when we arrived, we were hungry and Daphne set out in the night, in unfamiliar surroundings to hunt for food. No telephone to call a taxi, we were deep in the suburbs and it might have been the swinging sixties but for those of us who can remember the 1960s there were few supermarkets and convenience stores and they were not open at all hours.

We were in London for a couple of months when Don arrived. It was cold and the days were short. Don hated it. He went out a couple of times to listen to live music but could not stand the weather. This was the only time he would visit a country in Europe except when transiting to Nigeria in coming years. I have a number of letters written from Heathrow at times when he was travelling through. He had no interest in the UK or Europe. On this trip he booked himself the first ticket he could and sailed to Australia ahead of us.

It was Ghana and Kwame Nkrumah who helped shape Don's politics into a coherent shape around the relationships that existed between nations and countries around the world. He never lost his interest and in a scrap book of news cuttings from 1984 I found two articles on Ghana. One was titled "Ghana is 27 today" and appeared in *The Guardian* on the 6th March. The article outlines the austerity Ghanaians were suffering from, the spiralling inflation, fuel and electricity rationed and the downsizing of the public service. There was no byline and the reporter sadly wrote that Ghana would be celebrating the anniversary "noiselessly". On the 7th March Greg Obong-Oshotse wrote a longer piece, also in *The Guardian* titled: "Ghana a dream deferred". He wrote of the history of how Ghana had gained its independence after 113 years of the British. He said, "That day a dream was achieved and another born". He commented that on the 6th March Ghanaians, under the "irrepressible" Kwame Nkrumah could now embark upon the task of building a nation where there would be justice, freedom and equality for all. He also pointed out that Nkrumah's dream was even greater. Nkrumah wanted Ghana to be a model for Africa and a leader in establishing a United States of Africa. The Obong-Oshotse article finishes with comments on inflation and the daily earnings of most Ghanaians. By 1984 Don had spent about five years in the chaos that was Nigeria but he was still interested in Ghana and harboured a hope that the days of the dream were not completely over.

Chapter 6. The Flinders Years

Don arrived in Adelaide from Ghana, in 1966 and joined the new physics school in what would become Flinders University. The physics department was established in 1964 with Max Brennan appointed as foundation professor of physics for a new Adelaide University campus at Bedford Park. As the new buildings at Bedford Park were being prepared, the school was simultaneously established at the Adelaide University North Terrace Campus. This is where Don would work for his first months in Adelaide, moving to Bedford Park in July 1966. In March of 1966, the South Australian government passed the Flinders University Act. Under Professor Brennan it was decided the new department would adopt a school structure. As a new institution the university needed to establish a reputation and a research base. One strategy Max Brennan utilised was to secure "workshop facilities of a very high standard for the School of Physical Sciences and appointed skilled technical staff ".[1] On the chart below (Figure 6.1), that displays the structure of the physics school Don, as laboratory manager, is listed on the same level as the co-ordinating professor and the director of technical services. This led to some staffing issues. The two laboratory managers, chemistry and physics, were provided with a secretary each. This seems to have caused some squabbles at budget meetings with other staff members complaining about a lack of support services. In the budget meeting for the year of 1972 the diagram below was presented under 'Item 1.3 Secretarial Staff' and discrepancies in support staff were discussed.

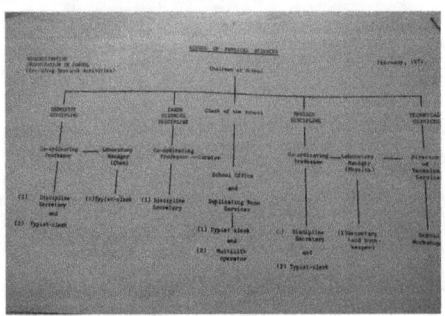

Figure 6.1. Structure of the School of Physical Sciences at Flinders University. Don was appointed laboratory manager and was allotted a secretary

I quote from the minutes:

> The disciplines of Chemistry, Earth Sciences, and Physics each have a Laboratory Manager, and the Laboratory Manager positions were established because of a) the organisational problems with laboratories, b) the considerable logistic problem with laboratory equipment and expendable items (chemicals, glassware, electronic components, engineering workshop store items), and c) the numbers of technical and laboratory staff to be supervised and administered. Each laboratory manager is entitled on the secretarial formula to ¼ of a secretary/typist. In practice Mr. Atkinson and Mr. Shearer completely utilise the services of two secretarial staff, and have done so from the establishment of the university.

Those at the meeting received an explanation about these arrangements. The rationale given was that the laboratory managers' functions were 'peculiar' to experimental sciences and:

> with a total technical staff of 48 and the immense organisational and logistic problem associated with laboratories, workshops, and technical staff, it is unrealistic to suppose that the laboratory managers would function without a full-time secretary/typist.

There was agreement that academic staff had experienced insufficient typing assistance to cope with their needs and the ratios of academics and secretarial staff needed to be increased. However, the laboratory managers would continue to have a full-time support person each. This was possible in 1972 because Professor Blevans was on study leave. How the positions were funded, in other years, is not known but Don continued to have a fulltime assistant. It is partly because of this assistance that many of the files I have accessed for this book exist and exist in reasonably organised form. Many of the papers had written on them, in Don's handwriting, the file where they belonged, for example, 'Gurindji file'. Someone went to the trouble of filing the papers and making comprehensive lists of all the papers in each file. The well-ordered documents have lost their order over the years and many are missing but it was a great foundation.

These files contained information on Don's years at Flinders, the electric car, the Gurindji campaign, Professor Brennan's plasma research and the Science and Society lectures Don initiated.

When Flinders became independent from Adelaide University there was a feeling in the air that this would be a university for a new era. The disciplines would not be in silos. There would be different relationships among them. Two problems existed that would make the breaking down of the subject barriers difficult. One was the geography at Bedford Park. The university had an artificial lake in the middle separating the sciences from the humanities and social sciences. Another was the decision not to have a student bar on campus so as well as being in an isolated place in the suburbs there was no obvious spot for students to socialise across disciplines. It was into this environment, where disciplines were physically separated, that the School of Physical Sciences established a series of Science and Society symposiums.

Apart from contacting the local communist party when he first arrived in Adelaide and starting to become informed about the growing anti-Vietnam war movement, one of the first political protests Don became involved in was the Metropolitan Adelaide Transport Study, known as the MATS plan. The campaign to stop the division of Adelaide by wide highways was one he threw himself into with vigour. This interest that Don had in 'liveable' cities and the role of science was one of the influences that inspired the Science and Society Symposium lectures. Another influence on the importance of science students studying the humanities and social sciences was the example of the Professor of Physics at Macquarie University, Peter Mason. Professor Mason had started general education lectures for physics students in 1967. These lectures combined history, philosophy and social sciences. Don appreciated Peter Mason's commitment to the social responsibility of science and followed his work closely.

Over a number of years, the Science and Society Symposium discussions at Flinders covered many topics. Volunteer lecturers from a variety of institutions gave talks on their area of expertise. The symposiums had a theme each term. Following on from the interest in the social responsibility of the scientist the topic for second term 1973 was "The scientist in society". Professor Rogers from the Waite Institute started the ball rolling with a talk titled, "What is science?" William Percy Rogers was a choice that fitted the world-view of my father. Professor Rogers was a serious scientist who was also concerned with the social implications of science and became increasingly worried about nuclear energy. He was also interested in education and youth and wrote non-scientific articles about science and education.[2]

In 1974, *On Campus,* the newsletter put out by the university, listed a new series of talks. The introduction to the advertised topics contained a comment on what a "popular feature" these Science and Society Symposiums launched by the School of Physical Sciences had proved to be. The talks took place on Wednesday each week, from noon until 1.00 p.m. The theme for the term was "The development of new technology" and speakers came from assorted institutions. Mr F. Gnatenko was the first speaker. The topic of Ted Gnatenko's talk was "Effect of large-scale technology". The institution he was associated with was General Motors Holden (GMH). Ted Gnatenko was a well-known union activist with the Australian Engineering Union (AEU) and he had helped establish a 'rank and file group' at GMH against the wishes of management and the Vehicle Builders and Employees Federation (VBEF). He would be sacked later in the year by GMH and the case of his dismissal went to the High Court.[3] Don was the fourth speaker in that particular symposium series and I have mentioned his paper, "Technology and its effects on the third world" in chapter 5. The last speaker for the series was a friend of Don's, Dr John Coulter. John was working at the University of Adelaide and spoke on "Alternatives to big technology". A medical researcher John Coulter was interested in conservation and the environment. He was a councillor on the Campbelltown council when he gave his address to the Flinders symposium and would go on to become a senator in the national parliament from 1987-1995. He was a member of the Australian Democrats. He would eventually resign from the Australian Democrats in 2001. He believed they had moved away from their democratic origins. These symposiums are one example of Don's involvement with the intellectual life of the university beyond his work in the physics department.

A special aspect of his years at Flinders that he found rewarding was the opportunity to work with younger people. Among the letters Daphne received at the time of Don's funeral was one by Nonie Sharp. Nonie, a long-time friend, with her husband Geoff, had been a founding editor of the magazine *Arena*.[4] *Arena* has been an Australian independent Marxist journal since 1963. Nonie wrote in her letter:

> Don had a strong sense of the possibilities of the human condition, and one way I'll always remember and keep thinking about him is his interest in the young and their possibilities.

A number of younger people Don met at Flinders were the PhD students. Among the students some would become friends, he followed the careers of a number and had an influence on some. One of the social activities Don enjoyed was meeting up with like-minded people for drinks and talk. Bob Lloyd, one of the PhD candidates remembered: "Don used to host us students at The Tonsley, or one of the other nearby hotels, on a regular basis, as I am sure you are aware." I was aware of this as I went to Flinders as an arts student in 1970. The Tonsley was a popular place given the lack of a bar on campus in those days. The Tonsley hotel had been built in 1966 as a watering hole for workers at the nearby car plants and the year 1966 coincided with the new university being established in the area. The pub was a popular haunt. Phil Nitschke refers to the 'conversations' in The Tonsley in one of his Gurindji letters on file. I believe some of these sessions were extremely lively.

Many of these research students were also connected through the nature of their research. Arriving at Flinders University as a new professor, Max Brennan decided to pursue plasma research and built a strong research group around him. This was done by combining a group of academics and doctoral students into a team that would study aspects of plasma as "the raw material of controlled hydrogen fusion – the peaceful counterpart of the H-bomb's menace". Professor Brennan developed the aim: "to build linear plasma sources that used a hydromagnetic ionising shock wave to produce highly ionised plasma at low cost".[1] Don always took an interest in the Physics graduates and a number became involved in the plasma research being carried out. Brian Bridger cited the following names at my father's funeral. Bob Lloyd, Rod Boswell, Drew Krix, Herb Stock and Phil Nitschke. I am sure there were more as I remember one who was a close family friend, Peter Christiansen. The research conducted by these doctoral candidates are examples of the research connections that existed within the university as well as an interest in social and political issues that involved a view of the scientist in society. The first physics PhD to graduate from Flinders was Peter Christiansen. Peter had started his studies at New England and then moved to Adelaide with his supervisor Harry Blevins. Peter's PhD study was "Properties of helicon waves in non-uniform cylindrical plasma" and he would go on to have a university career. Peter and Don had a previous relationship as Peter had been in Armidale at the same time as Don. Peter had come from Queensland and Don was a friend of his father. Peter was a reader in physics at the University of Sussex when he tragically died at the young age of 51. His research interests had remained focused on plasma physics. Peter and Don shared many political views and Peter was one of the people Don would meet at the Tonsley Hotel for a drink and discussion. Other doctoral candidates that met at the Tonsley were Rod Boswell, Phil Nitschke and Bob Lloyd. I am sure there were many more. Rod did a thesis on "A study of waves in gaseous plasma" and was a student radical. When the student magazine, *Empire Times*,[5] was started in 1969 Rod bought a press and printed the publication from his living-room in an attempt to avoid censorship. He went on to become a leading research professor at the Australian National University (ANU). Bob Lloyd was studying "Electron scattering from atomic hydrogen" and Phil Nitschke wrote his PhD on "The structure of normal ionizing shock waves". Those involved in the plasma research created a "ten foot long plasma source to heat hydrogen gas to about 40,000 degrees Centigrade so that it reaches a plasma state". As an engineer involved in the project Don was part of the team that tended to this plasma source. A story about the plasma research, titled *S.A.'s Part In Bottling Nature's Violent Fuel*, appeared in *The Advertiser* in January 1969. The report was written by science writer Barry Hailstone. The image below (figure 6.2) appeared in the paper and the legend below read:

> A bank of high voltage capacitors that can be charged to 8,000 volts to supply the 15 field coils spaced along the plasma source which form a magnetic bottle to contain the plasma. A door to the

room in Flinders University's School of Physical Sciences is fitted with a safety switch which discharges the capacitors when a person enters the room. In the picture is Mr. D, A. Atkinson, an engineer associated with the project.

Figure 6.2 Don working on the bank of high voltage capacitors a which was part of the plasma source research at Flinders. The Advertiser, January 18th 1969, page 25

Another of those who drank at the Tonsley and remembers Don's role in encouraging students is Ken Smith who is now a member of the Australian Electric Vehicle Association (AEVA). Bob Lloyd put me in contact with Ken when I was trying to find out what had happened to the electric car built at Flinders in the 1970s. Ken wrote:

> Don was an advocate of Solar Energy in the early 70s. He set up an honours project for me in 1973 working on "Heat Losses from Solar Heat Collectors". He even arranged for me to give a paper on this at an Australia New Zealand Association for the Advancement of Science (ANZAAS) conference at Flinders. There was an interest in wind turbines then too. A couple of experimental Wind Turbines appeared at Flinders behind the engineering workshop. This interest was inspired by the sudden increase in the oil price. But interest went away again in the following years (26.12.22).

Don would later take this interest in solar and wind to Nigeria. One of the PhD students at Flinders was a Nigerian man that Don met at Ahmadu Bello University in 1970. This student, Aako Ubabe was an undergraduate in electrical engineering when he met Don.

> I was lucky enough to have my final year project supervised by him; he taught me the value of thoroughness in the design and testing of electronic circuits. Forty years later (this statement was read at Don's funeral in 2007), the oscillator he helped me build is still functional.

Aako also became an important lifelong friend. He acknowledged Don's lack of religion but thought he had "the religion of service and commitment to improve the lives of all he came across". Aako recognised that such commitment could come with a heavy price. He also valued the relationship that developed.

> It is not an exaggeration for me to say that the single most influential person in my life has been Don Atkinson. I lost my father about the time I first met him; he became my father and my mentor. Perhaps I should further elucidate. I am a black African from Nigeria; Don and his family, white Australians. At no time throughout our long association have I, even remotely, felt this difference.

Two of the doctoral students mentioned above, Bob Lloyd and Phil Nitschke, are also mentioned in other chapters of this book as they became activists in the Aboriginal struggles that Don was involved with. Phil after studying medicine went on to establish *Exit International*. Bob had a successful academic career though it had a shaky start. Bob had gone to Strelley to work with the Pindan Aboriginal collective led by Don Mcleod and then accepted a job in England. Bob wrote to me:

> I finished at Strelley (chapter 9) in mid-1974 and took up a post doc position at Liverpool University. This position ended dramatically in November of that year when I was asked to work with the UK military on possible submarine detection using a laser I was working on. I resigned the next day, an event which appeared in UK and Australian media. At around the same time a strike was happening

at Flinders University where the students were protesting against the then vice chancellor, Roger Russell's involvement with the US military. Your father was involved in this action which influenced my resignation. Your father strongly supported my action in Liverpool and the strike at Flinders but the physics academic staff at Flinders were very upset about both.

Bob tells the story of his problems with military research in his recently published book, *A hundred years of insanity*.[6]

Student activism, for a good cause, always attracted Don's sympathies and these years saw student unrest, the Vietnam anti-war movement and strong union struggles. My sister Mayo and I had left home and were living in share student houses by 1970. I became active in the anti-war movement. Even at school I had belonged to a couple of radical groups, the *High School Underground* was one. Don could be quite a nuisance when I brought friends home. He would offer drinks and want to talk politics with them. There were evenings when a boyfriend would come to pick me up and we would end up staying home for the evening having drinks and talking to my father. A group of students and young workers lived around the corner from Don's house in Glandore. They called their share house "Uncle Ho's Cabin" and were part of the early anti-war movement in Adelaide. Don enjoyed their company and appreciated their activism. They were part of his extensive association with young left-wing people in Adelaide. These contacts represented a wide range of left-wing views from the Labor Party through to those who labelled themselves anarchists. Their activism and activities varied. Les Bowling, who lived in Uncle Ho's Cabin, was a Maoist and one of his more dramatic actions was to put barbed wire around the library building at Flinders University on one of the Moratorium days. Peter Hicks was a Flinders drama student who would do street theatre as Captain America. Peter managed to gain a huge amount of publicity at one stage by calling the press and declaring he would napalm a dog at the university. There was a strong contingent of anti-war protesters at the university across staff and students. Brian Medlin, the Professor of Philosophy at Flinders, was one of the well-known anti-war demonstrators in Adelaide and often in the media. The university had a religion centre that, at one stage, harboured conscientious objectors.

Don would appear as a character witness for protesters, arrested at demonstrations. He did this willingly but had to curtail this activity when one magistrate asked him if he was a professional character witness. He only gave support to people he knew and whose protest actions he supported but the magistrate managed to make his interventions less valuable by his implication that he was not giving genuine assessments of a person's character. Daphne would help those protesters as well. One day she was in court when my sister's boyfriend, Rory Mahony, was due to appear before the court. When his name was called there was no Rory. The magistrate said if he did not appear by the end of the session he would issue an arrest warrant. Daphne ran out of the court, waved down a taxi and went to Rory's place. He was still in bed. She took him back to the court. When Don was in Nigeria and writing his fortnightly letter home he would often ask about these young characters he had known and send them his regards.

In 1974, his sympathy for young activists and the Flinders Gurindji group (chapter 10) that he and Vic Barnett headed got Don and Vic into trouble with the university. It was August and a group of student radicals had occupied the registry in protest over compulsory history exams. The occupation took place in an environment of worldwide social unrest. The Carnation Revolution in Portugal that year heralded the beginning of an end to 40 years of fascism in that country. The year before, 1973, a coup had overthrown the Allende government in Chile. The Vietnam War had galvanised Australians in a way not seen before and anti-American feeling was strong. Many young people were questioning aspects of their education. At Flinders University, the disquiet came when the history department refused to negotiate on the position of compulsory exams. The students occupied the registry at the beginning of August. The Vice-Chancellor (VC), Roger Russell, the first American appointed to such a position in Australia, was out of the country. Those in charge of the university in his absence thought the occupation would soon be over so had decided not to ask the police for assistance. The protest was to be a month-long occupation that would become increasingly political as students started releasing the VCs private files about his research activities with the American military and his association with the American Central Intelligence Agency (CIA). After these files were made public funding of research and the role of the American military in universities became a focus of the protests. On the 28th August there was an extraordinary scene when some 400 academics stormed the registry building and except for skirmishes, the occupation was over.[7]

During the occupation, sympathisers to the protesters would supply resources and entertainment. There were films, discussions, performances. Don and Vic received an invitation to present on the Gurindji struggle. They went to the university armed with the trusty slide projector. During the evening, the power went off. Don went down to the switchboard and there was no seal to prevent him so he turned it on again. Later that night, after Don and Vic had gone home, the power was officially disconnected. The students then broke in and restored the power. Don and Vic were accused of turning on the power when there had been an authorised disconnection. They were suspended from work for a month while an investigation was carried out. I was with Don when the man from the university hand-delivered the suspension notice. It was August 23rd. Don said, "They've got you to do a dirty job". The man said, "Nothing to do with me Don" and literally ran from the front door. After the inquiry Don and Vic were reinstated. There was no evidence of wrongdoing. However, staff in the physics school had decided they would send Don to coventry. One man, a colleague and prior friend, came to Don's office and said he didn't agree with the coventry move and he would talk to Don when no one else was around. Don told him he was a coward and he could piss off. When the Head of School found out what was happening he called the instigators of the move to his office and told them to stop behaving like characters in an Enid Blyton boarding school book. This incident had an impact on some of Don's relationships with fellow staff members though, judging from the contingent at his funeral, he did not lose any of the people he considered proper friends. After the occupation no charges were brought against the students, although there were suspensions for a few. There had been strong support for the occupation from the student body as well as other universities around the country, some of whom attempted their own occupations.

Flinders had started the occupy movement before other universities which is why it lasted for a month. Monash students protested the assessment system in September of 1974 by occupying the administration building but after 8 days, the police charged. Seventy-four students were arrested. The charge brought against the students arrested at Monash was 'besetting a building' which carried a potential goal sentence of three months. Don was just getting to the end of his month suspension at the time of the Monash occupation and a friend, Barry, from Melbourne wrote:

> I presume you're back at Flinders now that your suspension has ended. Is the activity of the assessment campaign slowly dying down now that the end of the year is approaching? Activity here reached a high level immediately after the arrest of 74 people occupying the administrative building. Some two thousand students attended a meeting a day later.

The letter went into details about lies that Barry said were contained in the coverage in *The Age* newspaper. Barry claimed the meeting of the two thousand students had been misrepresented in the paper as the article in the paper said the students had rejected a motion to reoccupy the administration immediately. Mathieson (the vice-chancellor) was quoted in the paper claiming this refusal was victory for the "silent majority who rejected extremist action of a minority of militant left-wing radicals". Having reported this Barry dramatically said, "HE LIED". He then went on to explain in the actual motion that the students had voted for negotiations before the administration building should be reoccupied. These were fractious days and Barry's letter and Don and Vic's suspension are indicators of how feelings were running high.

During a life, there are decades where things seem busier than usual. These years were very full as Don was working at a challenging job, convening the electric car project (chapter 7) and making frequent trips to the Northern Territory to communicate with the Gurindji (chapter 10). He had also taken leave-of-absence and visited Nigeria for a year, returning to Finders in 1971. He still found time to explore his own interests and have a social life with friends and family. Lifestyle changes were in the air. In Armidale Daphne and Don had sought healthy lifestyles by activities like gardening, bushwalking and taking the 'youth drug' KH3 (chapter 4). Arriving in Adelaide in the mid-60s they found themselves in the decade of the big eat and drink. One feature of this was gargantuan business lunches. Don began to put on weight and suffer horribly from indigestion. Time for some changes. Daphne started packing healthy lunch boxes, business meetings were scheduled to be held during office hours. Simultaneously Don turned to exercise and cold showers. The cold showers I remember well. The theory was that a person should have a hot shower and then turn the hot water off for the last minute or two. I can still hear the 'brrrrs' that would echo around the house. One thing that did not suffer was his love of a drink and a chat. He did start to move from beer to wine and by the end of his life was an affirmed red wine drinker.

Figure 6.3. Don at a formal gathering on the 24th August 1974. He was only in the second day of his suspension. He is talking to family friend Gael Rees. Unwanted food from the event went to the students at the Flinders registry

As evidenced by the electric car project his attraction to alternative energy sources for the future, cleaner energy and travel deepened. Don started to ride a bike to Flinders but it was uphill and the hill at the end when he reached the university itself was a killer. He started designing electric motors for bicycles and making them in his shed in the backyard. He had a well-equipped workshop and a sign over the door that said, "Small is beautiful". I am not sure how many different motors he put together during this phase but he would later exploit this interest when volunteering as an engineer-in-residence at a local high school (chapter 11). Always the trickster he would ride along Marion Road, towards the university and when he saw another cyclist struggling a bit he would pop his motor on and sail past sitting back on his bike comfortably. Electric motors were rare enough in those days for him to fool many fellow cyclists. He was always pleased when the ones left gaping in his wake were young and fit looking.

Squash was another interest and he played a lot of squash while he was at Flinders. He had been sporty and played a bit of tennis when young and this had turned into a liking for squash. However, he started finding it hard to get partners because his squash friends became concerned that he might have a heart attack on the court. His style of playing was the culprit. As soon as the game started he would go bash, bash, bash at incredible speed, quickly winning the point. He would then prop himself up on his racket and gasp strenuously for breadth. It was disturbing to hear. He could win against most of his squash partners but over-time they did not want to play with him because they were worried about his health.

The major changes he had introduced into his life were a bit more activity and healthier eating. Adelaide was an easy place for good eating, as the central market must be one of the best in the world. Saturday was the day to go to the market and Daphne and Don would come home with bags of fresh food, cold meat, cheese and bread. Visitors would often pop in at lunchtime on Saturday knowing there would be great things to eat. He managed to balance his love of the good things of life with the health changes he was making. He was disappointed when he visited America towards the end of the 1970s and caught up with some of the colleagues he had worked with in Nigeria. He came back complaining they had all got skinny and didn't drink anymore. Where was the fun!

Conferences, professional organisations and being a union representative were all pursuits he took seriously. Ken Smith noted that Don organised for him to deliver a paper at an ANZAAS conference on Ken's solar energy research. Don wrote papers for conferences, enjoyed exploring the ideas of others and was an enthusiastic presenter. He belonged to international organisations like the *International Solar Energy Society*. He was in the Australian and New Zealand section. In local associations he would be active and was often listed as an office bearer. He was the registrar of the *Australian Institute of Science Technology* (AIST) and in this capacity was an advocate for technical training and the promoting of standards of competence. The institute welcomed technicians from all branches of technology ranging from architectural and survey drafting, to biology, mechanical engineering, electronics and many more. The institute had five aims:

1. To promote the standardisation of examination and the National recognition of Certificates for technicians
2. To promote technical education in the field of scientific techniques
3. To promote the recognition of the status of technicians
4. To provide technical information for the benefit of the profession
5. To promote the above activities on a national basis, by the establishment of Divisions of the Institute in all States.

Membership was open to all laboratory technical staff, including those working in engineering workshops and membership awarded according to educational qualifications and/or skill and experience. Courses at technical colleges across Australia, were being assessed and added to the list of appropriate qualifications accepted by the institute. In the July meeting of the AIST in 1970 a number of Tasmanian qualifications were approved, there was a guest speaker and a paper on technicians by D. Gadd was to be discussed. These issues of national standards, status and promotion of the importance of technical staff was significant. That there has been slow progress in gaining the recognition the AIST aimed for was illustrated in 2002 when Dr Ken Gadd (not D. Gadd who was Australian) of the Royal Society prepared a report for the *Association of*

Science Education.[8] The same problems of standards and status face still prevailed. The recommendation, cited below, could have been crafted at the AIST meeting in 1970 instead of for the ASE in 2002.

> Technicians in schools and colleges have a vital role to play in the provision of high-quality science education and, if they are to play this role to the full, all technicians must be supported in their work and accorded the professional status they deserve. Clear job descriptions for all technicians, linked to a national career structure and pay scale are required, as is substantial investment in technician continuing professional development.

Don was always loyal to his profession, was proud of his work and saw technicians as an essential part of scientific activity. He was involved in a number of committees to promote the sciences and physics, generally as well as advocating for better technical training. He participated in the preparation of physics papers for the South Australian Public Examinations Board (PEB) and was on the advisory curriculum board for further education in South Australia. He became distressed at the political interference in further education he observed over the years and thought something valuable to Australian society was diminished by the technical education sphere becoming a political football. He was not a luddite and continued to participate, as a student, to update his computer knowledge to the end. He maintained his stance on the potential of science to help humanity. The episode of the student occupation and the government withdrawing funding from the electric car project (chapter 7) were two events that would help define these years. He went back to Nigeria and decided to resign from Flinders in 1976.

Chapter 7 The Australian electric car

The electric car project that saw a group of engineers produce a car at Flinders University seems to have started around 1972 and by March 1973 was advanced enough in the design to be awarded a grant from the state government.

Looking through Don's files it would appear that the idea of an electric vehicle was being explored as early as 1968. There are a large number of newspaper cuttings, magazine articles covering different topics about the design features of electric vehicles over the years. In the file there is information on motorcycles, a go-kart (marked "this has potential"), photos of two-seater vehicles and vans from around the world, characteristics of the printed motor, application of plastics to special bodies, battery-powered bubble cars designed in Czechoslovakia being driven in Amsterdam and revolutionary battery research being conducted at Monash university. John Bowker, a pioneer of electric car research from the 1940s to the 70s, claimed a major breakthrough in lead-acid battery design.[1] At the time he talked of how he and his partner wanted to find associates to use their new battery to build a "peoples" car. Advantages of the battery include; "discharge at a constant rate over a considerable time span without any drop in voltage, the battery can be quickly recharged without damaging the electrolytic plates and can go through up to 900 cycles "before significant cell decomposition takes place." What I was most struck with was the comment about the people's car. This seemed to be the same zeitgeist that Don and his team were working in at Flinders University. A small, clean car for city use was the aim. This impression is supported by another article in the file from 1972. It was in *The News* and reported that the Asthma Foundation of SA was offering an award "to encourage the production of a relatively pollution-free vehicle for city use".[2]

One article appeared in 1968 that Don had carefully filed with a "noted" comment and a hand-drawn circle around the date. The article was a spoof and the fact it came out in April in the *Road and Track* made Don assume it was an April Fool article. It was called "Electrophant: Sheer audacity combined with superb engineering".[3] That this article was carefully copied and stored in the research file suggested it appealed to

Don's sense of humour. It was written by Tony Hogg. "The Electrophant, as its name implies, is an electric elephant, and to those of us who are familiar with the advanced technology of today, it is the logical solution to the current pressing problem of urban transportation". Hogg goes on to give a thorough analysis accompanied by photos, descriptions of design points and a range of models. "Miniphant has transistorized circuitry, Racing version is shown with earbrakes actuated". There are data, graphs and details of the road test. An enormous amount of effort went into this fake. I can see why Don found it funny and clever. Such findings in the files are a reminder that he tried never to be pompous or take himself too seriously. Such traits probably helped him keep perspective when important projects, like the electric car, were thwarted.

The electric car group at Flinders University consisted of three initially. Don was the convenor, an electrical engineer and laboratory manager in the School of Physical Sciences. Other members of the team were Darryl Whitford, an electronics engineer and Graham Woods. Viv Rush and Kevin Rush, both mechanical engineers, were also involved from fairly early in the project. In early press stories Don, Darryl and Viv are mentioned as the core team. However, Graham was mentioned as being one of the first three. Bob Lloyd, who had a doctorate in atomic/molecular physics, joined the project in 1975 and helped to model the performance of the car using first an old analogue computer at Flinders. Later a hybrid analogue/digital system was used that Don discovered at Adelaide University. The work on the car had started in earnest in 1972 after widespread consultation about the project. In a video[4] made about the car after the state government had approved funding Don discusses the beginning of the initiative and the people they spoke to before applying for grant money to develop the car. He explained that the car started as an experiment to try to address the problems of electric cars already being developed around the world. When asked about why existing electric cars did not meet requirements Darryl Whitford replied:

> Two basic reasons. One that they tend to be very heavy for their size. This is because the only viable source of energy is the lead acid accumulator and the fact that when they are used in urban conditions, where you experience a lot of stops, starts per mile and accelerate to

a reasonably high speed in between the range was so slow they were virtually useless.

Enthusiasm was enormous according to Don as they looked at problems, designed possible solutions, researched and prepared a presentation to the South Australian government. They consulted engineers, economists and sociologists. The car was not only revolutionary in design but the aim was to provide the public with an affordable clean vehicle. Darryl Whitford again:[5] "Society has come to the point where the car is a social necessity. This electric car will give SA a big chance for the future."

Elements that made the car different from others was a printed circuit electric motor while most of the vehicles around still coupled a Direct Current traction motor to the road wheels. In the Flinders car the printed circuit electric motor could convert to a generator when the transmission system was acting as a break. This would then automatically start to recharge the batteries.

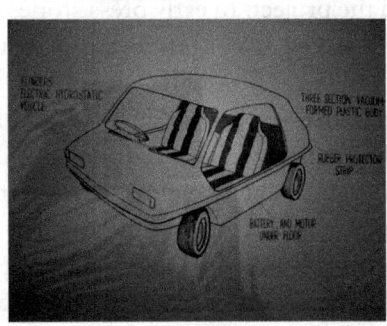

Figure 7.1. Early drawing of the electric car

A special lightweight low charge battery was used for the car. Trevor Ford[6] explained how the battery worked.

The battery current requirements are greatly reduced, resulting in a much lighter, more efficient battery. The electric motor is a printed-armature type which runs at constant speed throughout the vehicle speed range. High efficiency regeneration is used when the vehicle is retarded, resulting in increased range.

The regeneration is obtained to zero vehicle speed and can produce marked deceleration, the degree of regenerative braking being controlled by an 'accelerator' in the normal manner. No electrical control is used to govern either the output power or the regenerative power as the printed-armature motor determines its own requirement from the battery when used in this concept.

The teams' arguments were successful and in March 1973 the SA government announced a grant of $22,000 to build a prototype.[7] As described above the prototype would involve a printed-circuit electric motor, hydraulic transmission and long-life, low-weight batteries.

Figure 7.2. Road and Transport Minister, Geoff Virgo, delivering government funding check to Don Atkinson March, 1973

The successful funding arrangement with the SA government through the Industrial Research Institute of SA Incorporated attracted much attention. It is worth noting that to keep costs down the group convened by Don had agreed to donate their services to the development of the car. They decided there was a need to employ one senior technician and the rest of the money would be put towards building and testing the prototype.

In the next year the publicity and the interest attracted by the car was enormous. There was local publicity with the car appearing at the Royal Show. Don wrote an article for the SA Science Teachers Journal[8] while local papers provided a number of stories. The international response to press releases about the car were impressive. The Australian Information

Service sent out an article, prepared by Don, to embassies around the world[9]. The news release described the car, its purpose and plans for the coming year which were to road test the prototype and sub-contract to have another 6 cars produced as a first step towards exploring the idea of commercial viability. The news item was accompanied by a picture of Don standing by a graphic of the car. The team were confident that computerised driving comparison tests on simulated roads suggested the Flinders car could accelerate faster than existing models and had a greater travel distance on a standard electric charge. The responses came from around the world. The familiar picture of Don with the drawing of the car appeared in papers across Asia. Thailand, Bombay, Singapore and the Malaysian Sunday Times. The press officer, J. Stone, continued to send press cuttings as they came in. In June he commented: "Enclosed are further press cuttings on your electric car project. This time it seems you are big in New Zealand and Thailand. By July/August there were more cuttings from *The Straits Times* citing the High Commissioner in Kuala Lumpur and another Malaysian paper called *The Sin Chew Jit Poh* and another from *The Bulletin*. From the Philippines there was an article in the *Zamboanga Times*.

Figure 7.3. One of the photos of Don that appeared in the international press

The French Embassy contacted Don to express interest in November and wrote to ask to be kept informed. "Following our telephone conversation of today, please find herewith an article published in the French newspaper *Le Monde* dated 31st October, 1973. The Swedes were also interested in exchanging research and sent an article published in *Teknisk Tidskrift* on the 17th November. The Netherlands *Rijdend Nederland* (Driving Netherlands) carried a two-page article on the Australian car on the 28th November.

The interest continued into 1974. Businesses in the USA and Israel were wanting to know when the car would be on the market. Pedr Davis wrote the car up for *Popular Science*[10] and approved a design approach that was more inclusive than just concentrating on the battery. He agreed there were two radically new concepts introduced with this design, the constant-speed printed-circuit motor and hydrostatic drive. Such attention was affirming. Local outlets also kept providing exposure.

By 1973 Flinders University was already displaying components of the car, the first public appearance of the car parts occurred at the Royal Adelaide Show. At the same time as the first components were exhibited at the Show the Science and Society lectures, arranged by Don and others through the School of Physical Sciences, featured a talk from Mr Pike of the Australian National University (ANU) on 'Historical aspects of energy use by mankind". The theme of the third term lecture series for the symposium that year was energy and fuels. In February the electric car was featured on the front cover of the *Bulletin* of the Institute of Mechanical Engineers. By April 1974 the prototype of the vehicle was on display at a special exhibition. This was part of Australia's first exhibition of electric powered vehicles[10]. That electric vehicles were of interest to the public was evidenced by the thousands who made the trip to Bedford Park, south of Adelaide, to see the displays which included lawnmowers, golf buggies, wheelchairs, cars, tow-tractors and forklift trucks. From the photographs of the day the Flinders electric car received considerable attention. The copy of *On Campus* that covered the news of the exhibition also featured Don's lecture for the "Science and Society" course on "Intensifying the poverty of the world's poor". I link the Science and Society lectures to the electric vehicle project as both Don and Darryl expressed a wish to build a car that would support the common good and help ordinary people. The science of the electric car had a strong political and social underpinning.

By the end of the year, December 1974, the first stage of the project was nearing completion. Registered and ready to be tested as a short-haul commuter car Don would drive it home from work and park the strange looking vehicle in the street outside his suburban home. An innovation expected to be very important for electric vehicles was the introduction of a fuel gauge. This had been reported in the *Advertiser* on October 2nd 1974 and the writer Bob Jennings was at pains to explain the gauge which would indicate to the driver how much energy was left in the batteries.

> The gauge measures the specific gravity of the electrolyte in the battery by testing its refractive index, and automatically compensates for temperature, which vastly affects battery performance.

In November of that year Don gave a seminar on "Roads and Transportation Policy for Metropolitan Adelaide". In this seminar he discussed the crises in our cities and the environment. He raised doubts about the role of engineers who many consider to have brought benefits to people through affluence and contrasted this with those who are more circumspect about technology. He saw the possibility of a small electric car that could support urban structures "so that future developments and use of resources promote community growth and reduce feelings of alienation, isolation and despair".[11]

Figure 7.4. The Investigator Mark 1 December 1974. Driver Kevin Rush and passenger Darryl Whitford

Attacks on the idea of a widespread adoption of an electric car were another challenge for the Flinders group to face. A report by the Bureau of Transport Economics questioned many of the claims made for the advantages of the electric car and difficulties in a transition to battery powered transport. Among the criticisms were that they might be quieter on suburban streets but would be noisier under freeway conditions. They would cause unemployment in the oil industry, their weight would increase wear and tear on existing roads, omissions of carbon monoxide would diminish but there would be an increase in sulphur oxides. The lower performance of the car was also likely to cause accidents and they would be more costly than conventional cars. This report appeared in the *Advertiser* and Don was approached by the paper to comment on the criticisms. He first put the report in context by pointing out that the report was 12 months old and much of the material quoted in the report even older. Bringing attention to a conference that had been held at the beginning of the year, under the auspice of the Bureau of Transport Economics, he commented that the Flinders group had participated in the conference and from the quality of papers presented at the conference it was obvious that thinking had developed over the past 18 months. The pessimistic reviews written up in the newspaper had not been reported at the conference.

He then went on to refute the four main criticisms levelled at electric vehicles. These were the increase in sulphur oxides, the noise the vehicles would make on freeways, higher tyre and battery wear and unemployment issues in the oil industry. In relation to sulphur oxides he stated that Australian coal was low in sulphur oxides and power stations could control emissions. Recharging batteries should also be part of research into renewable energy sources like solar and wind. In terms of weight the Flinders car was designed to be about the same as a small four-cylinder car and should have similar noise characteristics. He thought battery cars would be more stable as the weight of the batteries is between the wheels and the unemployment argument was illogical. He pointed out that the petroleum industry was not something that could go forever and changes would be required in the industry.

I have spent time on the above article and rebuttal as it stands out among the many positive papers that appeared about the Flinders car in 1973, 1974 and 1975. *On Campus* June, 1975 had a summary of some of the reactions still coming in from around the world. Some wanted to order a car for themselves, some were inquiring about producing the car in their own countries (Portugal was one) and a Singapore company wanted to be the sole distributor for Singapore and South-East Asia. One from closer to home was an Australian pensioner who wrote in offering to drive one of the prototype cars as a promotion. She could not afford to buy a car but thought the idea great and she would really like to acquire one. The local papers were also enthusiastic. The car was written up in *Border Watch*, a Mount Gambier paper, as the car was to be exhibited at the Mount Gambier show. *Border Watch* still exists and is one of the oldest of the country newspapers, The *Hill's Gazette* had a cheery article called "It's 'go' for electric car". Don and Bob Lloyd presented a conference paper in April of this year, titled, *The Flinders Electric vehicle concept*. The paper is on ResearchGate but there is no indication of what conference it was.

By the beginning of 1975 stage 2 of the project commenced. The next step was to put a more powerful electric engine into a conventional light weight car body and build a number of prototypes. The Investigator Mark 11 had an adapted Fiat 127 body with a manual gearbox and front wheel drive. The body of the Fiat was not modified and the battery pack was under the bonnet with the "black box" instead of a four-cylinder engine. This car had range of 60 to 150 kms, depending on the number of stop/starts and it had a top speed of 65 kph. Battery costs to recharge were estimated at 30 cents and battery life was 600 cycles. It was hoped that money would be forthcoming for 10 more cars that would undergo intensive testing and necessary modifications could be made. The Flinders University electric car group believed they were on the threshold of success and the reaction to their earlier design supported this. The July 1975 edition of the Royal Automobile Association journal the *South Australian Motor* featured the car [11]and Darryl Whitford on the front cover.

> A feature article in the same journal finished with the words.
> There is more work to be done before the Flinders University care is ready for large scale production. Which means it is unlikely you will be able to buy a commercial version of it from your friendly neighbourhood car dealer next year, or even the year after.
> But if the car of the car of the future is electrical, it seems possible

that the Flinders may hold the answer.

Figure 7.5 Front Cover "South Australian Motor" July, 1, 1975

Figure 7.6 Feature article on the Flinders electric car in the South Australian Motor. July1, 1975

It was not to be. In August of 1976 the SA government pulled their funding.[12] The State Transport Department had put $102,000 into the project and although satisfied with the way the project had progressed the Minister (Geoff Virgo) said there would be no more funding. He blamed the Federal government saying the research and development funds had been drastically cut by the Fraser government for this sort of research and money had to be channelled into more urgent areas. This was a disappointment as the Dunstan government had progressive ideas and was against urban sprawl and the electric car should have suited these inclinations. Whatever the thinking Don was not discussing it with the government. Daphne answered the phone one morning and said Don

Dunstan was on the phone. Don Atkinson's reply, "Tell him I'm busy".

At the time the funding was pulled Don said the team had enough resources to continue until December but the group would then have to be disbanded. He was regretful that the synergy the team had developed would be destroyed and he pointed out to the journalist that "there has never been a greater need for an electric car both in terms of energy conservation and reduced pollution in our cities". Darryl Whitford told the reporter: "If we don't get the money, the whole thing will disappear and there is no way it will ever come back." Don resigned from the university on August 2nd, 1976[13]. He cashed in his superannuation and started making plans for future activities. He remained connected to the car project for the rest of the year. He stated in his resignation:

> I would like to remain convenor (unpaid) of the Electric Vehicle Group until the end of the year culminating the present grant from the Department of Transport. (I have discussed this matter with the Chairman of the School.)

That the Flinders electric car group were operating in an international environment was evidenced by Darryl Whitford's planned activities for the rest of the year. In September he was to represent the Standards Association of Australia at the International Electro-Technical Commission in Dusseldorf. The purpose of this meeting was to plan recommendations for a world rating standard for electric vehicles. He was also booked to attend a symposium in Germany, an energy conference in England and had visits to French and British manufacturers to discuss design and how to improve components. Darryl was the only one who stayed with the project.

Flinders did continue with the project but the emphasis was totally different. An agreement was entered into with a commercial company, Electric Vehicle Developments (EVD) and Darryl was the convenor on the university side. Darryl was interviewed for the *Sunday Mail* in 1979.[14] He described his earlier experience as "he caught a tiger by the tail when he got involved in the development of the Flinders University electric car". By 1979 he was the convenor of the Flinders car project but was working in conjunction with EVD to manufacture vehicle conversion kits. When asked what he would have done if he had not got involved with the original electric car group he thought he might have gone into bio-medical engineering. He also suggested he might had gone to work in the 'developing' world as the other two members of the first group had done. Don Atkinson was in Nigeria and Graham Woods was in Fiji. He commented that the Federal government seemed interested in electric vehicles for commercial use but he was still convinced that demand for small electric vehicles would outstrip that of commercial vehicles. It was a long journey from the heady days of 1972, when the excitement was palpable, to 1979. The arrangement between EVD and the university received government funding in 1980 and continued to 1985. A number of Bedford vans had been converted but these were eventually all returned to petrol motors.

Returning to the political situation around the car and why the funding was ceased for the small family car, there are a number of possibilities. The Whitlam government was elected in 1972 and the Whitlam government was determined to develop Australia's natural resources under a national policy that would benefit the country. It was in this political climate that state funding of the electric car project was commenced. In 1975 the Whitlam government was sacked and Fraser became the prime minister. Although socially progressive Fraser was economically conservative. The 1978 budget of the Fraser government, under Treasurer John Howard, sought parity for the pricing of Australian oil with the import market. Whitlam's Petroleum and Minerals Authority (PMA) was dismantled. In the decades since the 1970s foreign corporate influence in Australia and foreign ownership of Australian resources have become more pronounced. Today we have no robust standards for mandatory fuel efficiency. Australia has become a dumping ground for vehicles that are costly, less efficient than their overseas counterparts and increase pollution. This issue started in the 1970s and continues to be a problem today. It has been exacerbated through successive Liberal and Labor governments. A lack of political will is a major barrier to fuel standards and to the increase in supply of electric vehicles. This latter is important as Australian consumers are once again, like the 1970s, showing an enthusiasm for affordable electric cars.

Against this background I look at the Dunstan government in the

1970s. Dunstan was happy to abandon the Metropolitan Adelaide Transport Study (MATS) when he took office in 1970. According to Llewellyn-Smith (2012)[15] ,Dunstan was a bit of a micromanager and happy to intervene in decisions made by other ministers. He had proposed a satellite city should be built near Murray Bridge (Monarto) that would represent the latest thinking in urban and social planning. The purpose of this was to prevent Adelaide becoming a huge urban sprawl as its population expanded. Proposed in 1972 the idea never eventuated, though land was acquired, the idea was finished by 1976. The estimated population explosion by the beginning of the next century also failed to happen. Another plan that did not fly under the Dunstan government was applying new technology to the public transport system. By 1976, when the state government pulled funding from the electric car project the economic environment had changed. The Fraser government was embarking on a strategy to privilege private interests in the development of the Australian economy. Fraser stated he wanted to direct resources away from government and into the hands of private investors. There would be tax cuts, industry would be protected so it could be competitive again and there was the usual attack on regulations as red tape. Did this Federal environment impact on the Dunstan governments ability to enact reforms or support initiatives like attempting the commercial production of an inexpensive electric city car? Adelaide was built on the automotive industry. Was the concept of a small Australian electric car too great a challenge? According to an article in the left-wing newspaper *Vanguard*[16] written in 2021, by 1976, when the SA government cancelled funding to the Flinders electric car group Dunstan had a new advisor. This advisor had previously been a director of General-Motors Holden. The article cites Don Atkinson as commenting on the attitude of Dunstan's new advisor to electric vehicle research in Australia. Don was reported as saying the following about the new advisor:

> We understand he has said that Australia is incapable of carrying out this sort of research. He considers that the only way a viable electric vehicle could be developed is 'within the structure of the existing internal combustion vehicle industry'...If this is the sort of advice the government is getting, no wonder the electric vehicle project was axed.

The SA Transport minister had blamed Federal cuts in research for initiatives like the electric vehicle being taken from the state budget. Given the Fraser governments attitude to the private sector and Australian resources it is understandable that Federal funding was no longer supporting projects like the electric car. Don Dunstan's government had a reputation for championing civil liberties, equal opportunity, anti-discrimination and Aboriginal land rights, this was a progressive government. National parks and wet lands were protected and the 1975 container deposit legislation was legendary. There may not have been any strong commitment to issues of energy sources and future problems of pollution that would be caused by large numbers of petrol cars on the roads. We cannot know the reasoning behind the decision to stop the electric vehicle research in the form it was heading. After the Flinders group broke up what was left of the project went on to build a converted car and Bedford vans that went to government departments. As mentioned above these were later returned to petrol motors. A far cry from the affordable, small car for Australian workers.

When researching material for this chapter I came across two videos on youtube[4] and there was Don's father's face and he was explaining the Flinders car. The videos had been posted by the Australian Electric Vehicle Association (AEVA) and they had discovered the original cars, Investigators Mark 1 and Mark 11 that were made almost 50 years ago. A member of the association, Bruce Tonkin, now owns the cars and is restoring them so they can be displayed to the public as part of SA's electric vehicle history. In 2021 he made a comprehensive presentation to the AEVA SA/NT branch[4] about his conservation work on the car and explained elements of the original design. To bring the car to the public is an act that seems in the spirit of the original project. Life is full of coincidences and Bob Lloyd, from the electric car group in 1975, was recently taken to a farm site near Mt Barker where Bob was able to view the Investigator Mark 1 and talk to Bruce about the restoration. These two incidents mean I can now fill in some of the gaps of what actually happened to the two cars. My sister had been told that the Investigator Mark 1 had gone to the Birdwood Mill Motor Museum but had been destroyed in a fire. She visited the museum and was told they did not have the car and there had never been a fire. Bruce Tonkin, the member of the AEVA who is now restoring the two cars filled in the blanks[17].

The Investigator Mark 1 was loaned to the Birdwood museum and the electric motor was placed in the Investigator Mark 11. Both cars were sold in 1986 and after going through two different owners Bruce bought the cars in 2014. Bruce decribes the condition of the Mark 1 and the assistance he has received from original members of the team:[15]

> By 2014 the vehicle had been sitting for nearly 50 years, empty of all fluids and sometimes left outside and so was not in very good condition. Since coming into my possession I have removed rust, repainted, replaced pipes, hoses and fittings and reupholstered torn seats.

He goes on to detail how Darryl and Viv Rush have helped in resurrecting this 1970s phenomena.

> Viv Rush, mechanical engineer, who helped with some machining of parts for the restoration and has provided original construction notes, photographs, video and has identified the parts from other vehicles that were used.

> Darryl Whitford, electrical/electronic engineer who has been most helpful in telling me how the drive system is supposed to work, how to achieve adjustments of that system and fault finding when things go astray.

When I started this chapter, I did not expect to experience the type of interest that has been expressed about the electric car project in the 1970s. Don would like this as the electric car was an important part of his identity as an engineer. He was despondent when the funding ceased and moved on to other adventures but there was always the niggle of what might have been. Viv Rush seems the only one of the original members of the electric car team from the 1970s who is still involved in an alternative car project at Flinders. There is now a Flinders Automotive Solar Team (FAST) that has existed since 2016, there is an Investigator Mark 111 and the team concentrate on the *Bridgestone World Solar Challenge*. This is a 3000 km race that starts in Darwin and finishes in Adelaide.

Figure 7.7. Final report on Stage 1 of the electric vehicle project. Image provided by Bruce Tonkin

Figure 7.8. The Investigator Mark 1. Photo courtesy of Bruce Tonkin who is restoring the car for the Australian Electric Vehicle Association

Chapter 8 Nigerian experiences

Daphne and Don first went to Nigeria in 1970 and stayed through 1971. Mayo and I had left home, Margaret was sent to boarding school and David accompanied them. David went to the staff school, that is the school for children of staff at Ahmadu Bello University (ABU), Zaria. Don had taken leave from Flinders University. He was being careful to hedge his bets this time. When Daphne and Don first arrived they borrowed plates, cups, cooking bowl and a tea pot from the Estate Department of ABU. The invoice, dated 4th August, 1970, provides a list of items loaned. They were free for the first 4 weeks, one pound for the next 8 weeks and if they had not been returned after 12 weeks the borrower must pay the full amount of the articles and could retain them. They were returned to the store in June 1971.

Don went into the chaos that was Nigeria with a very different frame of mind than he had when he went to Ghana. He later described himself as "an outsider who had a feeling of obligation and strong attachment for Nigeria".[1] The feeling of wanting to help was still there but now he was acknowledging his enjoyment of Africa in its own right. There is plenty of evidence that Don worked hard and there were some dark moments but he also managed to party. He was living on the campus and had plenty of colleagues to spend social time with as well as having opportunities for political discussions over drinks. A pastime close to his heart. From one of the letters he wrote in August 1971 his feelings could almost be considered a love/hate relationship. On the first page he waxed lyrical about one of the gates in Old Zaria, the Northern Gate and talks about the ghosts that you can imagine descending. He then moves on, in the letter, to describing how he and Daphne enjoyed a night out at a dance hall with colleagues. They were sitting "outside to get away from the music. Under a clear sky adjacent to some magnificent mangoes and a row of eucalypts". On this occasion they were accompanied by colleagues from the graduate studies department, veterinary science and agronomy. The discussion was about the IMF (International Monetary Fund), the World Bank and the 'Green Revolution'. The latter being an initiative of the Nigerian government that had replaced the 'Feed the Nation' initiative. The discussion was not only scathing about the IMF and World Bank and the manipulative role these institutions played in countries like Nigeria there was also criticism of the type of research produced at the university in relation to food production in Nigeria.

The letter goes on to describe some of the South Americans from Brazil and Chile he met at the university. At Flinders University he had played an active role in the series of Science and Society seminars. In this letter he was trying to refine his ideas of the role of the university, state and society and the influence of different environments. An understanding he gained from the experiences of his South American colleagues is the idea that an economy can grow while poverty can also increase. The letter has an enthusiastic section on the advantages of microelectronics which may be a left-over from his "small is beautiful" phase but also a reaction against some of the giant international projects that Nigeria was paying for that he could see were not even providing water, sewerage or affordable electricity for most. In this letter Don discussed the unions. A national case had just been through the courts and factory workers had won a minimum wage of 125 naira per month. The university staff was presently considering industrial action for more pay. University lecturers started on 800 naira per month. Don commented that for the first time in his life he was seriously thinking of voting against strike action. We obviously were not writing letters as he finished somewhat plaintively "Where is Mayo? What of the Adelaide tribe?" This chapter is largely based on letters and this letter is an example of the range of issues he talked about in his letters, the glimpse of social life, the highly political environment he was enjoying and his appreciation of the physical environment.

Figure 8.1. The familiar blue aerogram letters that would arrive each fortnight

Below is postcard showing an aerial photo of Ahmadu Bello University. As the university grew the compounds where the staff were accommodated were further and further, often kilometres, from the main campus. As new compounds were added there were long waits, months or years, for services like a reliable water access to be organised. This was significant for the last contracts Daphne and Don had at the university. They found themselves on the outer edge of the campus, writing their letters by candle-light until they rigged up some battery systems and were without water when the wells nearby ran dry. When my grandmother visited they had to acquire a car as she could not walk miles in the African heat or cope with the local buses.

Figure 8.2. Aerial photo of Ahmadu Bello University. By the time Daphne and Don left in the 1980s there were a lot more buildings. Daphne has numbered some of the buildings 1 – 10 with black texta though they are a bit difficult to see. Water tower, 2. Assembly hall, 3. Electrical engineering, 4. Mechanical engineering, 5. Civil engineering, 6. Estate management, 7. Institute of health, 8. Student colleges, 9. Sick bay, 10. With arrow to indicate this side of the campus contains the catering flats, club, swimming pool and staff school (where David went). There seems to be an 11 but must be a mistake.

My sister Margaret was still in high school and Daphne and Don flew her over to Nigeria for Christmas the first year they were in Zaria. They had planned a full timetable of excursions and were happy to be sharing their life with a member of the family. One anecdote Margaret remembered was a bar in Kano that they sometimes frequented. A group of musicians would entertain the drinkers. They did not play instruments but would get a guest to sing a song and then repeat the rendition exactly. Margaret said after a few drinks she and Don were happy to join in. They sang "My grandfather's clock". The version sung back to them was hilarious. They musicians sang it exactly as they had heard it with all the flat notes and other mistakes.

Local arts and crafts had been a strong interest while Daphne and Don were in Ghana and this continued. Not long into their first stay in Nigeria Daphne and Don became interested in some of the local artists. In 1996 they wrote a letter to my son reminiscing about their time in Nigeria and included some photos of their favourite memories (figures 8.11 and 8.12). From the images there is evidence to suggest that many of the highlights of their experience in West Africa lay in the observing traditional life and history of the country.

Figure 8.3 David with a local artist and a painting bought by Don

When Don had moved to Adelaide from Ghana he had already developed a strong interest in alternative energy. He and Daphne had been part of the anti-nuclear movement in the 1950s and 60s and he was also concerned about sustainable life styles for all. In Ghana there had not been time to develop his interests to any great extent but Flinders University provided a useful home to develop his ideas. Arriving in Adelaide he was lucky to meet a group of PhD students and others who were stimulating company as he continued his exploration of science and how it could serve society. This group, described in chapter 6, were important influences in Don's work life. He wanted to build things that worked, were sustainable and accessible to the Nigerians without the manipulation of external interests. The following pictures are indicative of the type of projects he undertook. There was increasing frustration at lack of resources for these types of initiatives during the years he worked at ABU.

Figure 8.4 A solar panel with batteries and leads to conduct electricity to a pump with an electric motor.

Daphne and Don were back in Adelaide by 1972 and in this year a young PhD student, Aako Ugabe, came to Flinders to study. Having met Aako in Nigeria Daphne and Don were friends when he came to Australia as an international student. Aako completed his PhD, married a fellow doctoral student, Kanchana, who was researching English literature. They returned to Nigeria to work and raise a family. In subsequent visits to Nigeria Kanchana and Aako were close friends and remained in touch for the rest of my parent's lives. Don went back to Nigeria and Aako and Kanchana were able to give him important social support. He also had some Ghanaian acquaintances who had fled Ghana after the coup and were now working in Nigeria. From 1975 to the mid-1980s Don worked in Zaria, making regular trips home. Politically Nigeria was a very different country from Ghana and as Don was involved in life in Nigeria for so many years I have added an historical timeline of his Nigerian years. The Biafran war was just finishing when Daphne and Don first went to Nigeria and during the years Don worked at ABU there were coups, an assassination and a second republic was established for a while.

1970	January 8th	Ojjukwu fled into exile. Phillip Effiong acting president Biafra
	January 15th	Effiong surrendered to Nigerian forces and Biafra reintegrated into Nigeria
1971		Nigeria joins Organisation of Petroleum Exporting Countries
1973	January 22nd	A plane crashed in Kano, Nigeria, killing 176 people
1975	January 29th	General Yakubu Gowon was overthrown in a bloodless *coup*. General Murtala Mohammed became Head of State.
1976	February 13th	Mohammed was assassinated on his way to work. His deputy, Lieutenant-General Olusegun Obasanjo, became Head of State and set a date to end military rule
1979		Shehu Shagari won election to the Executive Presidency of the American-style Second Republic.
	October 1st	Shagari sworn in as president
1983		Shagari won re-election
	December 31st	Shagari government lost power in palace coup
End of second republic
General Muhammadu Buhari became head of state and chairman Supreme Military Council of Nigeria

1984	April 17th	The Buhari regime promulgated Decree No. 4, the "Public Officer's Protection Against False Accusation" Decree, which made it an offence to ridicule the government by publication of false information.
1985	August	Buhari was overthrown in a palace *coup*. General Ibrahim Babangida became Head of State and President of the Armed Forces Ruling Council of Nigeria.

Figure 8.5 Historical timeline. Source: Wikipedia²

After the first trip Don did not return to Nigeria until 1975. He was always keen that members of the family would share the experience and in 1977 Mayo and her partner at the time applied to go to Nigeria. Mayo's partner, Phil, had a PhD in mathematical modelling and got a position at ABU in information science. Unfortunately, Daphne and Don were back in Adelaide when Mayo and Phil moved to Zaria but they were able to help Mayo and Phil to settle by introducing them to their friends and helping with the university Estates Department and other useful information. The trip did not work out well. Mayo had been married when she was very young and not divorced her husband. The university was pressuring Mayo and Phil to legalise their relationship, Mayo wrote to Daphne asking was there anything she could do from a distance to organise her divorce. A second problem was that she had applied for a job at the American Embassy and this was seen as a hostile act. We all got letters, posted in London, to say she had been deported and put on a plane to Heathrow. She wrote these letters about her deportation while in mid-air. Luckily, her partner Phil had been able to contact his parents who had friends in London who kindly looked after her on arrival. In the end she stayed in London for a year and did a course at St Margaret's hospital. When she returned to Australia she moved to Melbourne and lived in St Kilda.

Daphne and Don continued to go backwards and forwards. In the late 1970s Don went back to Nigeria alone while Mum stayed in Adelaide for David to finish his high school studies. They both went back in 1981 and it seems to have been a particularly challenging year. In this year they were allotted a house which was not completed at the time of their arrival. Daphne and Don stayed at the university hotel and my grandmother, Annie, who had decided to make a long visit, slept at a friend's house nearby. When they moved into the new house it was on the far side of the campus, some kilometres from the university and they had no access to a car. Electricity and water supplies were unreliable, universities across the country were engaged in protracted industrial action to improve the lot of students and teachers and there were food shortages. The icing on the cake was that Don had a bag stolen with his passport in it and had to start the onerous task of trying to arrange a replacement passport from Northern Nigeria where there was no consular support. Poor Annie complained that she was feeling the heat but Don said it was no worse than Sydney in summer. He thought she was suffering culture shock. He wrote he felt sorry for his mother as Nigeria was not her scene. Most of her reasons for disliking the place he thought reasonable but he hinted that a tiny bit of her dislike was lodged in Annie herself.

Don reported he was working hard and says it was a tough time for most as:

> Uncertainty about H_2O, NEPA (National Electricity Power Authority), transport, housing, chemicals exhausted in the department for printed circuits, getting used again to improvising string instead of microprocessors. It all takes time.

He was teaching a group in a work experience program with no hook-up wire (single strand insulated wire), one reel of solder and three soldering irons. He had 15 students in the program. He thought this was a tragedy as most of the students were very keen. The only thing that was in abundance was chalk and as Don was always a Deweyan and believed in 'learning by doing' this was anathema to him. This is relevant to the union industrial action that was taking place at the same time. When Don was in Nigeria in 1971 he had not been enthusiastic about striking for more pay for academics. This struggle ten years later seemed to have been largely about the students and the exploitation of casual and student staff. A typed 8-page single spaced letter was sent to New Nigerian

Newspapers Ltd on the 10th October of 1981 giving a comprehensive description of what the industrial action in the universities was about and some of the opposition the union was facing. The letter was written by the national president Dr Mahmud Tukur of the Academic Staff Unions of Universities (ASUU).[3] On responsibility for the unions actions he thought the primary responsibility lay with the government which "is the body ELECTED by the Nigerian people and entrusted with the progress of the country and the welfare of her people". He pointed out that the current action of the union in not starting the next teaching session was both "a moral and historical duty we owe ourselves, our students and the nation. Student ratios, exploitation of non-permanent staff, the problem with academic freedom if academics are integrated into the public service". The country was undergoing current austerity measures and Dr Tukur explained that the universities were so far below austerity measures that in many departments it was not possible for academics to carry out their teaching duties. Dr Tukur stated the union action was an acceptable and acknowledged one.

> All we are doing is to use, with the greatest of decorum, the only weapon at our disposal, a weapon recognised throughout the modern world – the temporary withdrawal of one's service.

Don was supportive of the actions and when the government tried to declare the action illegal on the 13th October he was strongly in support of the union's refusal to call off the action. This confrontation between Shagari's government and the ASUU seems to have set the pattern for ongoing struggles for higher education in Nigeria. At ABU, when Don was working there, the leaders of the fight were Dr George Kwanashie and Professor Abdullah Mahdi. On this occasion Dr Kwanashie[4] addressed the ABU staff and called upon the branch to "display a sense of maturity and balanced judgement" and as "far as the union is concerned, its action complies fully with the laws of the land as they pertain to industrial disputes". He finished his statement to the branch by urging "all members to remain steadfast" and "ignore any directive not coming from the National Executive of the Union".

There are various mentions of the strike in both Daphne and Don's letters. Mainly to comment that the strike was still on and it was causing difficulties in getting bank remittances sent back to Australia. Daphne and Don had underlying financial problems all their adult life. They were not profligate but certainly generous. When he could not find supplies Don would often buy lab equipment himself sooner than have to rely entirely on chalk, or bits of string, when working with the students. Every house they ever owned had a couple of mortgages on it which is why it was important to send money home. Daphne would complain about having no money for her interests. Daphne's interest was craft and her hands were always busy with crochet, tatting, embroidery or knitting. Beginning in Ghana she developed an interest in the textiles and beads of West Africa. On her birthday that year Don wrote:

> Daph's birthday yesterday – no fancy chopsticks dinner; a piece of chicken with pepper sauce served the needs. She did find one of the old traders in the morning, so guess what? Yes, Morgan got it – she has another necklace – a Jacob's tear, two malachite beads, some agate and a few harder to define stones. We suspect the whole necklace may have come from East Africa.

When we had to pack up after Daphne died she had the biggest collection of trade beads and textiles I have ever seen. She could have stocked an entire market stall. She had started the collection in Ghana in 1965 and had bought some superb examples of different types of beads and cloth over the years.

Figure 8.6 A sample from Daphne's bead collection

Their particular money issue in 1981 when Annie made her protracted visit was buying a car. Daphne and Don could manage by catching local transport and walking but Annie was 80 and housebound without a car. A Russian friend had offered Don a car, some Soviet version of a fiat. He wanted the money in sterling. Don cooked up a complicated scheme where some friends in Adelaide, Brian Bridger and Rick Burford, would sell the lathe and mill in his home workshop. He described the lathe and mill as his two great loves in his "small is beautiful" workshop. I was to organise with the bank to send the money to an account he kept in England. I cannot remember any of these events but looking through the letters for the year 1981 I find letters from Daphne and Don thanking Margaret and I profusely for lending the money for the car. They did get the car as I have photographs of it.

Don was employed as Visiting Chief Technologist, Department of Electrical Engineering at ABU. As well as participating in the strike, battling extreme shortages of resources he seems to have had a variety of responsibilities. He designed and put together a handbook for the department, arranged an exhibition at Enugu, former capital of Biafra, for the Science and Technology show, supervised post-graduate students, taught engineering courses and organised the laboratories. He enjoyed the Science and Technology show at Enugu and although there were still signs of the recent war Don liked the look of the town. The exhibition was well run and there was an enthusiastic public response. In terms of the people he worked with, the students and assistants, they seem to have come from all over. He describes his teaching, work environment and indulges in a trip down memory lane.

> I have two courses, a first year electronics course [remember our students do A level maths and physics for admission – approximately 1st year uni standard in 63] and a Part 11 Measurements Control course. The first will have 120 students and tutorials, the second will have about 20 students. The first year failure rate in engineering is catastrophically greater than 80%. Will be assisting in a service course to Part 11 Chemical Engineering students. It has just occurred to me that I have been doing electrical/electronic work for forty years. I thought I needed a change, in a way that is what I had for the last two

+ years. Being back amongst scientists where the boss is a Marxist and at least the staff talk and argue politics (a wide spectrum) as well as the detail of their profession gives me a comfortable feeling. It is a bit like meeting someone from Sydney who understands the fourpenny rush of the Saturday pictures, summer swimming in the canal and being chased along the railway by railway detectives.

He goes on to talk about his job in more detail which gives an insight into Don's approach to his work.

> Practical job. A. Supervise and train would-be technicians in the art of servicing electronic equipment ranging from simple meters to fairly complicated (1978 vintage) computer and microprocessor equipment. Emphasis on logical systematic break-up approach so folk are not over-whelmed. Replacing some guide sheets.
> Main job. B. Establishing a printed Circuit Technical facility in a hostile environment. Keeping detail log on this and bringing people along, step by step hopefully so they will understand pitfalls and alternatives. No post 1970 electronics possible without this. We have some very big obstacles to overcome.
> Chairman of new laboratory course panel. C. Our laboratories are obsolete. Initially they were set up by a team under the Chief Engineer of the BBC (K. R. Sturley). This gives me a unique chance to implement ideas on engineering training I have developed over the last two decades. Caution required as it is so easy to become gimmicky and jump to use of latest components in a comic book fashion without students gaining a gradual feel of underlying physical world without the bewilderment of unrelated change.
> A funny job. D. I am in charge of all purchasing and stores staff. This is an area where corruption is very prevalent. Goods are signed for and never seen, unaccountable burglaries always happen when attractive items arrive, customs officers offer naira for a signature and the goods are wheeled out a back gate and so on. It is not chicken feed as we spend 200,000 naira (80/81) (about 400,000 dollars). Since 1978 not one major consignment of electronic components has made the road from Kano to Zaria. This fractures all teaching

efforts.

While in Nigeria Don became enamoured with the attempts made by those engaged in craft labour to build an industry. He was keen on the work that was done in Jos[5] and started his own collection of Jos pottery. At some stage Don was involved in meetings with the Kaduna Industrialisation Committee. An activity that he described as "a festival of masochism". The so-called senior technical partners in assisting in the development of West Africa (the USSR, USA, UK, Germany, East and West, Rumania and Bulgaria), he felt were determined to set up non-sustainable industries where resources had to mainly come from Europe and the breakdown of essential parts were inevitable. He also thought little attention had been given to the existing craft industries and some would even be displaced in the proposed changes. These were similar issues he had encountered in Ghana.

Figure 8.7 Examples from Don's Jos pottery collection

Nigerian painters and the lens they took to the country was also an interest. As early as Don's visit in 1971 he was seeking out local artists. The picture below is a wonderful portrait but also sad as the artist had to paint the picture on a piece of scrap paper and the typing on the other side can be clearly seen. The artist signed the portrait, James Reese, Katsina, which was then part of the Kaduna state of the Nigerian Federation.

Figure 8.8 Portrait done on recycled paper so the typing on the back can clearly be seen

Figure 8.9 Better quality paper available for this painting of Ibadan, capital of Oyo state

Daphne and Don also went further afield in their travels as is attested by this ink on cotton painting that references Yoruba mythology and possibly came from the Oshogbo school.

Figure 8.10 This is one of a pair. I do not know what happened to the other one

This year was difficult. Living conditions were tough and Daphne and Don were without water for months at a time and then suddenly they could water the garden and had fabulous pressure. As Don was working at an enormous pace, not having to queue and lug water was always a welcome relief. Aako and Kanchana gave them a television though I gather the content was pretty scatty and they often did not have power. It was the radio that kept Don going in relation to contact with world affairs. He had rigged up a battery system so he could usually get some kind of news. He could often get the BBC, thought the USA and USSR stations were insulting and occasionally could pick up Radio Australia. In one letter he admitted to having just enjoyed a stimulating show from Radio Australia but did admit he wondered if it was an especially good once off as he had so little access he could not really comment on the overall quality of Radio Australia. We heard no more about the strike that had been frequently mentioned in 1981 but by 1983 he was mentioning another possible strike. With 6000 students and no water for toilets and at one time no finances for food for the students, there were times when the university could not operate.

There were successes as well. With a colleague, Professor Buba Bajoga, Don had worked on a syllabus that he considered would lay the foundations for solid technical engineering programs at ABU. Don and Buba were expecting opposition from other staff but found support amongst the people they had most expected to oppose the changes. One outcome was that Don was invited to a conference in Benin to present on the reconstructed African engineering prospectus at ABU. He managed to set up the four-year program he had wanted for years and some of his students did extremely well in exams and their research. For Don these were the rewards he looked for.

By 1983 the Nigerian experience was becoming more challenging. Don was becoming increasingly aware of having close family on the other side of the world and a mother who was aging. This led to some serious soul searching about when he would come back to Australia and had he managed to achieve anything in his years in West Africa. One worry was that although he had some great colleagues the climate was against sustaining the changes. Without equipment, enough staff and a commitment to work in problematic circumstances he was not sure he was leaving any legacy. He felt that once he went the work he was doing would disappear and he hated the idea of giving up. He was disappointed thinking that this was his last chance to build something and the environment was so difficult. The letters through this year increasingly requested the family send books and components. As the post was so unreliable every time a friend left Nigeria they were asked to post letters. Nursing friends of Daphne's visited them in Nigeria during the year. Chris, my husband, was asked to get books from the Adelaide University Bookshop to give to the nurses to carry even though Don usually tried to avoid giving travellers books to transport because of the weight. I was sent into the city to buy electronics components and even my 8- year- old son was asked to source a recent copy of *Electronics Australia*. Daphne always asked for a particular red hair dye. She wore her red hair as a badge of courage and said she was not prepared to go grey in Nigeria. The brand she was using was only available in Australia and in particular shops.

As the year of 1983 wore on the political situation became more heated. Shagari had won the election early in the year but except for increased electricity supply during the election period most agreed the political climate was declining. Don had a group of friends that loved to drink and talk politics. Some were Nigerian colleagues while there were some Ghanaian exiles amongst the group, work mates from various countries and a group of young academics recently graduated. There were two bars on the campus where they usually met, the staff club and an unofficial bar run at the front of a friend's house. The year continued with problems with water and electricity supplies, food shortages and high prices, a bad Harmattan season and then, in the middle of the year, one of his closest friends and colleagues, Patrick, had an horrific accident. Patrick was from Sierra Leone and had a reputation for being totally charming, a womaniser and heavy drinker. Patrick was one of Don's main supports in the labs. At first Patrick was not expected to survive, then it was thought he would be a paraplegic but he gradually started to recover. His wife organised a roster in the hospital so for weeks friends sat with Patrick twenty-four hours a day until he was able to leave the hospital. Daphne and Don were both rostered on. It must have been difficult for all. Daphne said that Patrick was not a good patient but then admitted he had horrific injuries and the hospital did not have any pain control medication. When Patrick left the hospital Don would spend time with him every day. This was a double whammy as Don was time challenged as well as missing Patrick at work who was his main partner, apart from Buba, in the teaching labs. In the end Patrick went to Bulgaria for intensive physiotherapy.

By the middle of the year there were signs of change that would augur the coup in December. Don's friend Bala[6] (Yusufu Bala Usman) gave a workshop titled: "The Odama report and the real causes of the current economic crisis". The Odama report was produced in February 1983 by the National Economic Council. Bala summarised six characteristics of the Nigerian economy identified by the committee and questioned whether they were problems as designated by the committee or constituted a crisis. The problems were: a) most state governments on the verge of bankruptcy, b) smuggling and tax evasion so bad they impacted on internal revenue generation, c) hoarding at home and abroad impacting on monetary transactions, d) acute unemployment, e) support for private investors had led to a low rate of productivity and f) dependence on imports and "increasing paralyses of the governments' capacity to monitor, control and plan the economy". Arguing the country was in crisis Dr Usman found the recommendations put forward by the economic council were superficial and ignored basic structural elements of the Nigerian economy like the relationship with "the capitalists of Western Europe and North America and the people of Nigeria, and their human and natural resources". The people of Nigeria were "an essential source of the generation of wealth by plunder and capitalist investment" by these capitalists he declared.

The coup happened in December. The coup was announced on the radio and the announcement was repeated across the day. After a day of repetitive announcements with no information Don and Daphne headed to their informal bar. At the bar there was consensus that a coup was not a good thing but the increasing chaos of the Shagari regime made any change welcome. By the time people went home from the bar they had still heard little news about what was happening and who was in charge. There was a curfew, Daphne and Don were a distance from Samaru, where the main university campus was and they felt isolated in an information vacuum. Daphne said she and Don were talking around in circles when one of Don's closest friends, Abubakar Siddique Mohammed, a lecturer from the Department of Political Science and International Relations and another friend walked into the house and accepted beers. As Siddique arrived he was "declaring it to be a wonderful day and the best organised military coup ever experienced in Nigeria". The chaps drank beer and there was a jubilant feeling to the evening.

A month after the coup Don would write that Bakari, the coup leader, was little more than Shagari, the ousted leader, in uniform. The euphoria at seeing the last of Shagari quickly dispersed for ordinary people. The currency was changed to try to get rid of hoarding and all overseas assets had to be declared. People were sleeping outside banks to try to get their savings. The queue at the ABU bank was at least half-a-mile according to one witness on the first day. Those with contacts were trying to get their money out the back door.

Don's friend Bala came to see him one night in May, one month after the Buhari regime promulgated Decree No. 4, the «Public Officer»s Protection Against False Accusation Decree", which made it an offence to ridicule the government by publication of false information. Bala was being taken to court accused of making a critical statement about "rogue chopping money from a reafforestation program in Sokota and Bauchi". He was being sued for 500,000 naira for damages. He was denying the charges but was naturally worried. I do not know what happened in this case as further letters did not return to this incident. Bala seems to have survived the crisis because looking him up on the internet I found he worked at ABU until his death in 2005 and seems to have had a successful career. Don reported in his letter about Bala that repression was getting worse and moderate newspaper editors were now in goal. He said the situation at the university was tense as the student population were divided in their support or opposition, to the new regime and some academics were stirring the pot. In particular he was critical of four Polish members of staff. He had previously banned two of these Polish technicians from the laboratories he was in charge of as they were dismissive and rude to the Nigerians. All were Solidarity supporters and he decided that they were "elitist s—ts".

Daphne and Don had now gone backwards and forwards to Nigeria for 14 years. They had made some dear friends and Don was in two minds about whether he wanted to leave for good. Daphne had no doubts, no water for most of the last year they were there was a killer. They talked about doing one more round at ABU, after a break in Australia, but Don had a heart attack and it took him some weeks to get back to work, even half time. While he was recovering Daphne had a severe case of malaria. She got over it but had lost so much weight Don said if you touched her you would cut yourself. I think they missed the country for the rest of their lives. In 1996 they wrote to my son, Morgan, who was completing high school. They did not know what to send him or what advice to give so they sent four photographs saying: "Some of the greatest experiences in our lives were in connection with our times in West Africa and we still get pleasure out of contemplating them". They had selected four photographs with a commentary under each. It seems a fitting way to finish describing this adventure.

Figure 8.11 The first photo is a dye pit used to produce blue-dyed baft. The middle photo is the Northern Gate to Old Zaria mentioned at the beginning of this chapter. The third is a pot-sellers place in the market

Figure 8.12 This man was making a hand-embroidered robe in traditional patterning for one of the local Emirs. The robe would take up to a year to make.

Chapter 9 – Involvement in Aboriginal struggles

There were no clearly defining moments in my father's life but many would consider his involvement in Aboriginal struggles one of the most significant. As discussed in chapter three it was through the Communist Party (CPA) and union movement that he gained many opportunities and a network to satisfy his need for activism. The CPA since the 1920s had expressed more reasonable policies in relation to Indigenous Australians than any other party in the country. Perhaps it was contact with the international communist movement and learning about struggles against colonialism and imperialism, and the rights of minority peoples that influenced them. Many in the union movement were communists after the war and the combination of political awareness and real-life battles gave impetus to their activism. This was especially noticeable in the fight for basic rights for First Australians where the unions, some Christian groups and political radicals tried to work together. Probably the most important influence in this area of Don's life was my maternal grandfather, Roy Ockenden. Roy and Don first encountered each other about the time Don met my mother in 1948. Daphne and Don were married in 1949 but as Roy was in the CPA he and Don might have met earlier. Roy's work was a major inspiration for Don in his later efforts to help the Gurindji in their fight for land rights in the Northern Territory. When Roy and Don met Roy was already a long-time supporter of rights for First Australians. He had joined the CPA in 1922 and knew Tom Wright (*New Deal for Aborigines*, 1939)[1]. Tom Wright was the president of the Sheet Metal Workers Union (SMWU) and was an early critic of government policies, both Federal and State, towards Indigenous people. He also attacked the church run missions. The reforms he called for in 1939 were a product of the time and would now be seen as inappropriate and not far-teaching enough but were radical for 1939. Roy and Tom Wright were both on the NSW Labour Council in the 1940s.

It was through the Communist Party and the union movement that Don was lucky enough to meet many Aboriginal activists and their non- Aboriginal supporters which made it possible for him to engage in the struggle for civil and political rights and social justice for First Australians. In this chapter I touch briefly on some of the influences and activities that provide a background to chapter ten which covers some of Don's undertakings in relation to the Gurindji struggle in the Northern Territory from 1966.

One of the non-Aboriginal friends of Mum and Don who was a strong supporter of Aboriginal rights was the painter Eric Putland. Eric had an important presence in our family because the painting (pictured below) was bought by my father before I was born and had always been on the wall of the family home, wherever that happened to be, until Mum moved into a retirement village in 2010. It was an unusual painting to find on the walls of a suburban house in the 1950s. The painting by Eric was bought by my father at the *Modern Writers Club* exhibition of Aboriginal art and literature in 1947. The date and price appear on the back. The painting cost my father 5 guineas which must have been the best part of a weekly wage at the time.

The *Modern Writers Club* exhibition of Aboriginal art was written up in the *Sydney Morning Herald* and the journalist who reported on the exhibition thought Eric one of the more colourful artists to comment upon. The article on Eric appeared under the title "Great Hunter Home Again." The correspondent who penned this piece described Eric as a picturesque figure, using capitals for the word PICTURESQUE and in the article went on to say Mr Eric Putland was a "famous Queensland shark fisherman, hunter, and bushman whose oil paintings of Aborigines' heads are attracting interest in art circles." The paper referred to Eric's adventurous life that included being a sailor, hunter and shark fisherman. An accident in Brisbane in 1942 left him with an injured spine and he left his "alligator hunting, his kangaroo shooting on horseback, and his wandering in small boats" to take up painting. He said he had chosen Aboriginal portraits as a focus for his paintings as a lifetime spent with Aboriginal people had given him an "absorbing interest" in the lifestyle. He was impressed with the Aboriginal men he had worked with as horsemen, sailors and cattlemen and thought as seamen they were amongst the "world's finest". He spoke in strong terms to the correspondent from the newspaper about the need for the white society to give Aboriginal people their "rightful place". He espoused the CPA policy that by rightful place he did not mean assimilation and expressed a desire for rural Aborigines to be given what would become a demand for land rights.

Figure 9.1 "Margar" by Eric Putland. Sold for 5 guineas in 1947

There were a large number of letters from the Putlands in Don's papers, though Eric seems to have been the main writer. These letters were mainly sent from places in the north, places like Cairns, Lightning Ridge and Walgett. In letters from Eric to Don and Daphne there is a shared interest for the advancement for First Australians as well as social and artistic ventures that left-wing activists pursued at the time. Aboriginal literature for a young audience was a topic brought up with Eric by Daphne and Don and they both suggested developing books with specific Aboriginal content for young people. Eric thought it was a wonderful idea but probably beyond them.

> About this matter of a book for the junior members of the Australian (and other) communities. This poses a problem. Do you really believe that I, or we, would be capable of anything of real value in that line? ... I can write jingles, I know the original Australians better than many men do, and I can produce drawings, paintings, and woodcuts as I produce letters or an occasional short story – in a crude uneducated sort of way. Neither of us has any illusions about

our joint or individual ability, and a book for kids would have to be solid and outstanding to fulfil its purpose. I think too that it would have to sneak past the bourgeois censorship of critics and such to reach a worthwhile audience. The job would be a joy ...

He also had a dig at a well-known cartoonist, known for his realist art saying if they did produce any children's stories we would have "none of his caricatures of dark kids". Eric said he himself had written a story about Sam Pootchamunka but it was not suitable for young readers. I cannot find any sign of this story but the cartoonist he referred is still reasonably well known. Years later when the Aboriginal artist Dick Roughsey and his friend Percy Trezise[2] started producing good quality Aboriginal story books for children Don was thrilled to be able to buy them for his grandchildren.

Eric was a communist. This was not unusual after the war when many were seeking a better and more peaceful world. The concern about racism and First Australian rights in Australia had been an outstanding issue for many years. The CPA had been sympathetic to the Aboriginal struggle for rights since the 1920s and Katherine Susannah Pritchard, author of *Coonardoo*, was a founding member of the party. The left-wing network that came with being an energetic member of the CPA meant Don had the opportunity to meet many people he admired, Aboriginal and non-Aboriginal, who were part of the struggle. Daphne and Don lived in Kings Cross when they first met Faith Bandler who was one of the activists they would associate with through the peace movement in Kings Cross. They would go on to work with Faith Bandler in a number of organisations, including FCAATSI (Federal Council for Advancement of Aborigines and Torres Strait Islanders) and she was a dominant voice in the 1967 referendum when constitutional changes were made to include Aboriginal people in the national census and give the Federal government powers to enact legislation for the Aboriginal population. Burnum Burnum (Harry Penrith), the well-known Aboriginal activist and actor was a friend of the family, especially close to Roy. Burnum Burnum and his first wife Carmel Nelson lived in our Heathcote house for some months in the 1950s. After Armidale, when the family moved to Adelaide, activists like Glad Elphick became colleagues in the fight.

Don originally met Glad through the Aboriginal Advancement League and she went on to found the Council of Aboriginal Women of South Australia. There were too many good people in the struggle to name here. There were influences closer to home as well.

Daphne's family, on her mother's side, displayed attitudes that supported the idea that the treatment of Aboriginal people in Australia was unjust, prejudicial and hateful. The words 'prejudicial' and 'hateful' are taken from a poem by Daphne's Aunt Gwendoline Tidd. Gwen Tidd not only wrote poetry but she managed to get her poems published. For Don coming into a family that had a published poet was pretty impressive. Daphne's parents were divorced and Daphne's, also Daphne, went to live with Gwen after her marriage finished. Visits to Gwen and Daphne's mother were part of the family round at Christmas and whenever we were in Sydney. Gwen was a religious woman, a nurse who had been in Greece and North Africa during the second-world-war. She felt strongly about peace and war and what settler culture had created in Australia in terms of treatment of the original inhabitants as well as impact on the ecological well-being of the continent. Examples of her ideas can be found in a book of poetry, *Thoughts and thought,* which was published in 1972,[3] There was a poem about Albert Namatjira in the collection written in1969, the year of his death. One of the verses:

> What strength of moral courage
>
> To hold a force as this –
>
> While timeless ages mocked
>
> At white man's laws.
>
> His longing heart was weeping,
>
> A proud head bent in grief,
>
> While his spirit lived in "Dreamtime",
>
> With his ancient tribal race.

I found a copy of this poem in Don's papers. Gwen also had enormous respect for the ABC journalist Frank Bennett. Like Namatjira, Bennett died in 1969. He was supportive of Aboriginal rights and was a witness to the Gurindji strike in 1966. Gwen was so moved by his reporting on a case from Roma, Queensland, where an Aboriginal woman was convicted of causing her baby's death, that she wrote a poem. The first verse:

> Our conscience locks the mind,
> An Aboriginal baby dies;
> A mother pays in goal and scorn,
> Man's inhumanity prevails.

There is a statement under the poem saying that the case was later quashed in the Queensland Court. Gwen also wrote a poem to Bennett on his death saying: "For humanity and justice/ he lived and gave his life". Don would encounter many such influences to help him develop his conscience on the rights of Aboriginal people and the role of white Australia.

As mentioned the most important mentor for Don on working for Aboriginal rights was my maternal grandfather, Roy and this is where ideas and political activism merged. Roy had joined the CPA in 1922. He gradually moved away after Krushev's speech to the United Soviet Social Republic's (USSR) 20th party congress in 1956. It was ironic then that when Roy was visiting the family in Armidale in 1963 he was attacked, in the student newspaper, for being a communist. Roy had arranged to present at the Rationalist Society meeting at the University of New England on the 19th June. He was taking the opportunity to present on the Aboriginal struggles in West Australia while visiting the family in Armidale. He was a long-time supporter of Don McLeod and the struggles in the Pilbara. By 1959 the Nomad group under the leadership of McLeod had moved to Roebourne, eventually buying Strelley Station in the 1970s. Roy had visited the Nomads at Roebourne in 1961 and was using slides and lectures to inform people on the east coast of the conditions the Nomads were suffering as they tried to determine their future. An outraged member of the public came to Roy's defence when he was accused of being a communist and wrote to the *Nucleus*, the student paper on June 4th 1963[5] telling the readers grandfather was not a communist. Whispers of communism were common during the cold war era. The topic of the talk and that Don was one of the few open communists in Armidale help explain the attack. The following letter appeared in the *Nucleus* titled:

"McCARTHYISM"
Sir,
I wish to express my indignation that some "community-minded" people, in this University and outside, should try to prejudice the right of visitors to this University to be heard fairly. As is well known in the Western world, a person is guilty by association, and a person thus guilty can never get a fair hearing.
The case in point is the visit of Mr. Roy Ockenden – who, because of his activities in trying to help W.A. Aborigines has incurred the wrath of those whose gravy-train was rocked – he is therefore to be branded a Communist, despite the fact that his actions and sincerity show that he is certainly not. ... (the letter goes on to identify the meeting and attacks the whisper campaign mounted against Roy)
Yours in disgust, HUGH SPENCER.

The 1950s and early 1960s were challenging days for those on the left but Don could have see the humour of the situation and had filed the letter in his Armidale papers. The planned presentation highlighted Roy's commitment to the Aboriginal cause and this is something he and my Don were wholly in agreement on.

Roy was a close friend of the Marxist, Reverent Alf Clint,[5] who committed his life to establishing Aboriginal co-operatives with mixed success. The Reverent Clint had been converted to Christian Socialism by Father John Hope who donated a house to the co-operative cause that would become the TRANBY Aboriginal Co-operative College[6] in Sydney. TRANBY was a success and a constant in Roy's life. He was one of the trade unionists who helped Reverent Flint establish the college in 1958. The story in our family is Roy died at TRANBY. It was 1968, he was doing one of his slide shows on the Aboriginal land rights struggle when he suddenly sat down. He had had a massive heart attack and his last words were reported as, "I'll be fine in a minute."

There were many organisations Roy and Don belonged to, among the many, was The Federal Council for Advancement of Aborigines and Torres Strait Islanders (FCAATSI). Other organisations that, according to Roy's correspondence, he was involved with included:

- The Queensland State Council for the Advancement of Aborigines
- The Aboriginal Australian Fellowship (NSW)
- The Union of Australian Women
- The Council for Aboriginal Rights (VIC)
- The Original Australian Progress Association (WA)
- The Narrogin Native Welfare Association (WA)
- The Aborigines Advancement League (SA)

A number of trade unions supported the co-operative associations that would lead to the land rights movement and there are many letters to Roy from the Sydney Trades Hall in his papers on these issues. According to the *Aboriginal Welfare Bulletin* in 1963 twenty-eight Trade Union Councils across Australia had declared their support for the Aborigine Co-operative Movement. There were many other organisations not listed here that played a significant role in the land rights struggle. Some of these are mentioned in the next chapter which describes how Don formed a fundraising organisation in Adelaide to support the Gurindji at Daguragu (Wattie Creek).

Activism led Roy all over Australia. He was a keen bushman, a ranger in the Heathcote and Royal National Park, south of Sydney and was heavily engaged in the trade union movement. He was on the NSW Trade Union Council in the 1940s (figure 9.2). Daphne used to say that, "once Roy made up his mind about something you could never change him." This was probably a good and bad trait. He was certainly dogged in his pursuit of justice whenever he thought there was wrongdoing.

Over the years Roy and Don shared many memberships and activities in relation to First Australian rights. Common undertakings seemed to consist of visiting First Australian groups to collect information on living conditions, letter writing, especially to politicians, petitioning the parliament, educating the public, often through film or slide evenings and fundraising. Projects were initiated around housing, hostels, such as Kirinari for young students and support for co-operative initiatives like the Nomads co-operative in Roebourne, WA. There were of course endless meetings at local, state and national levels. The injustices the two became involved in ranged from individual cases to movements like the co-operative movement, fighting with the state for equal pay, job rights and land rights. Roy was an office bearer with the Aboriginal Advancement Society and one of the many cases that bothered him was one that occurred in Walgett. Two children, Roy Hickey and Fred Morgan, were removed from their parents for minor transgressions and taken to Sydney.[7] A campaign was launched with Roy and Don writing to the minister, F. H. Hawkins, for Child Welfare and Social Welfare. Don wrote he was, "appalled at the callous attitude shown by your department and the police in the handling of these children, particularly in the decision to separate them from their parents." He accused the department of deliberate discrimination. This letter was written on September 9th 1964. Roy wrote to Hawkins on the same day protesting the trivial charges against the children. He said in his letter:

Figure 9.2 Roy Ockenden at Richmond with fellow union delegates in 1953. Roy is in the front row, fourth from the left

I can only suggest that the poverty-stricken circumstances of the parents are due to the crimes of the white community against the Aborigines and that the action taken against the children is unlikely to react to their benefit."

On the 30th of September Mona Frame, from the NSW Aboriginal Fellowship at Trades Hall, wrote to Grandfather, saying a letter had been sent to the Premier and representations made to the minister. Mona stated that the mothers had not wanted their boys taken away. In early October Daphne wrote to the Union of Australian Women offering to organise protest letters to the minister. She also asked for specific details of the case for writers to include in their letters. Minister Hawkins reply to Roy's letter is undated, though professionally typed on official letterhead. The answer was obscure and intransigent. In September as a result of these protests the minister wrote, "the Legislative Assembly that the mothers of the two boys, aged 10 and 9, had asked that the boys be committed because they were uncontrollable."[7] That this was not the case is suggested by the letter from Trades Hall in September and the fact that Mrs Morgan, mother of Fred Morgan, met a delegation of Trade Unionists from the Builders Labourers Federation (BLF) in 1964 and told them she still did not know where her jailed son was.[8] I cannot find any further records of the case or if it was ever resolved. The tragedy was one of many.

Another case the three, Daphne, Don and Roy, got involved with occurred in Armidale. My family lived in Armidale from 1957 and the house we lived in was in Mann Street, East Armidale. Armidale was a town and gown place as it consisted of country people, squatters, a university, a teachers' college and two great public schools (GPS), using the English term of the word 'public'. Don deliberately bought a house that was as far away from the university as possible but still in the town. This was towards the east end and not far from an Aboriginal settlement known as "the dump" because of its proximity to the local dump. The dump was specified as a reserve under the Aboriginal Welfare Board in 1958. At that stage it was a collection of tents and humpies with no electricity, sewerage and only one tap that the local council could turn off at will. After a breakout of preventable diseases, that killed several children in 1960, the Welfare Board were forced to act. In 1961 the humpies were bulldozed and 14 corrugated iron homes, with no lining or hot water, were built. The dump was then dubbed 'silver city'. However, surveillance from the welfare officer and police if anything was worse than previously experienced when the settlement was still "the dump".

In October 1963 a local Aboriginal man had returned to his home on the reserve a bit the worse for wear. Roy, who was a teetotaller, knew the man and described him as 'likeable' and when drunk and he would go quietly to his home to recover. The local welfare officer (a man called Yates) and a policeman went onto the reserve, enticed Jimmy from his home and then charged him with being drunk on the reserve. He spent a night in the cells and was fined five pounds. He tried to get legal representation but failed. Roy was visiting Armidale at the time and approached his friends in Sydney for legal advice. A letter was sent to William Rigby, a member of the NSW Parliament who was known to Roy as a founding member of the "Aboriginal Australian Fellowship" organisation. Rigby replied on the 25th of November that he had written to the Premier who was the Minister for Police. The reply from the Premier was to request further details so the incident could be fully investigated.

A friend of Daphne and Don, Selma Stock, was the honorary secretary of the "Armidale Association for Assimilation of Aborigines" and Mum approached Selma. The issue had been clearly identified by Roy who posited the following questions to the Armidale group.

> Are police entitled to act in the above manner in relation to Aboriginal people? If so does their authority in this matter differ from that exercised over Europeans in similar circumstances? What is the best available redress if any?

Selma replied that the circumstances were not fully known, she was keen to know if the drinking laws had been altered and she was worried about the relationship between the police and the Aborigines. End of another frustrating story.

Figure 9.3 One of the humpies bulldozed in 1960

National Aboriginal issues were closely followed by Daphne, Don and Roy. The Pilbara strike in West Australia from 1946 – 1949 was a dramatic event in the history of Australia. This was the focus of Roy's talk to the Rationalist Association in Armidale when he was attacked for being a communist. Leaders of the strike were Don McLeod, Dooley Bin Bin and Clancy McKenna.[9] To support the strikers the Committee for the Defence of Native Rights (CNDR) was formed in Perth in 1946. The committee consisted of the usual suspects of communists, trade unionists, women's groups and church organisations. Enemies tried to dismiss the CNDR as a communist front but the committee was successful in publicising the events in WA to the rest of Australia and to the world. This publicity was invaluable. There was also a controversy in 1957[10] that helped bring general attention to the parlous state of Aboriginal rights in Australia. A film of the Aboriginal people of the Warburton Ranges was made and shown throughout the country by the Aboriginal Australian Fellowship Society. In Sydney the CPA newspaper, *Tribune,* reported that an audience of 1500 – 2000 had attended a showing of the film and there were tears and cries of disgust. This was one of the films that would have a profound effect on Paul Robeson when he saw it in 1960 during his tour of Australia. The other film was a short film titled, *People of the Pindan,* that publicised the Yandiyarra mining co-operative that had been set up in the Pilbara. This was established in 1949 under the guidance of Don McLeod.

The publicity from these two films was a driver for the establishment of the Federal Council for the Advancement of Aborigines and Torres Strait Islanders (FCAATSI). FCAATSI was set up in 1958 as an umbrella group for all the societies and associations concerned with Aboriginal affairs. Roy and Don were members of FCAATSI as well as being active in a number of the member groups. Roy was especially keen to promote knowledge of the struggles that were happening in the Pilbara. Roy corresponded with Don McLeod and by 1961 Don McLeod informed him that the efforts of Grandfather and others to stop the Social Services department from withholding benefits from the local people had been partially successful. There was also a growing difference between the Pindan and the Nomad groups. Roy decided it might be timely to visit the Nomads Pty. Ltd. Aboriginal Cooperative at Roebourne to "remain with the people and help in any way possible". He would only stay for six months as he found "I was neither as tough nor as clever as I thought." Our family spent Christmas 1961 together in Sydney.

Roy was busy the following year as TRANBY had its official opening. He also travelled to Queensland at the instigation of Reverent Clint to investigate a proposed project at Clump Point. He continued to publicise his WA experience and helped organise speaking tours for Dooley Bin Bin. While the Nomad people continued to fight the good fight, which was many layered and had lots of ups and downs, in the Northern Territory another dispute was blowing up that would lead to the Gurindji strike in 1966. Back from a disappointing year in Ghana in 1964 Don was ready to throw himself into the fray. By October 1966 Captain Major (Lupgna Giara), Dexter Daniels and Stan Davey were attending public meetings around the country. Frank Hardy's book *The Unlucky Australians* helped bring this struggle into the public eye. Don's role in the Gurindji fight for justice was another example of his activism.

Don's networks continued to expand and an important network by the 1970s were the student unions, many of them politicised by the war in Vietnam. Sometimes the organisations needed to be persuaded. When some of the physics post-graduate students approached the Post-Graduate Students Association at Flinders University to donate some of the union fees to the Gurindji campaign there was push back. Phil Nitschke, as a PhD candidate, led the skirmish and was attacked by a fellow student who sent a letter to all members of the association before the general meeting in August 1972.

> The Association is at present under siege by a self-styled anarchist, revolutionary, etc., Mr Phillip Nitschke … His current boast is that, with ten of his collaborators, he will change the constitution to allow for the issuing of political edicts and for the use of post-graduate money in supporting certain political movements.
> The first moves in this campaign are to be made at the next General Meeting (1/8/72). It is hoped that a mandate allowing the Committee to make political statements on behalf of its members. Once issued, the Agenda then includes the first motion of a political nature, giving support to the Gurindji in their struggle against the Federal government (a nice safe precedent-setting motion).

The writer goes on to say the meeting is to finish on a motion voting for a donation to the Gurindji and the writer scurrilously adds in brackets (The I.R.A. have been mentioned as the next recipient of Mr Nitschke's financial benevolence). Left-wing friends of Don and Phil, on the humanities and social sciences side of the Flinders lake, mediated this problem and the post-graduate student association became strong supporters of the Gurindji.

Don became a participant in numerous causes. One concerned the Aboriginal activist Kevin Gilbert. What appears to be the page of a Flinders University student newspaper, in Don's archives, involves the case of Kevin Gilbert. Don had approached the student group with a request from Kevin Gilbert to support him in a coming court case. The students agreed to help and wrote a half page article and included a petition.

Kevin Gilbert contacted Don Atkinson (Physical Sciences) last week. He asked if his story could be made known to people around Adelaide as the restrictions placed on him made it difficult for him to do so.

Kevin Gilbert is a well-known Black Australian artist, playwright, poet and writer. On October 19th he was charged with maliciously threatening the life of the Queen.

The case was important because Kevin Gilbert had been in goal for the murder of his first wife and was released on a 'lifer's licence' which made many forms of activism difficult. In the case of this charge, "threatening the life of the Queen", Gilbert could have been returned to goal for life. A support committee was formed in Sydney, anti-racists were approached and a petition was organised. Don, as an admirer of Gilbert's artistic work, politics and activism had been approached by Kevin Gilbert for support and he was happy to throw himself into the cause.

The Gurindji story is told in the next chapter. Don still remained in contact with those struggling in WA. Bob Lloyd, a long-time friend and a doctoral student, had finished his PhD at Flinders University and Don arranged for Bob to volunteer at the Strelley Community, near Port Headland, with Don McLeod's group. Bob was there in 1773/74. At one stage he flew to Wattie Creek with Jacob Oberdoo to deliver food and supplies to the striking Gurindji people. Bob took a post-doc in England after his stint with the Nomads in WA and when he returned to Australia he became part of the group working on the electric car at Flinders University for a while before resuming his academic career.

Chapter 10 – Supporting the Gurindji land rights struggle

> Poor bugger me, Gurindji
> My name is Vincent Lingiari, came from Daruragu, Wattie Creek station.
> Me bin sit down this country
> Long time before the Lord Vestey
> Allabout land belongin' to we
> Oh poor bugger me, Gurindji

Gurindji Blues song written in 1969 by Ted Egan and recorded by Galarrwuy Yunupingu, the recording of the song sold 20,000 copies and it financed the tent embassy in Canberra for its first six months)

> Gather round people I'll tell you a story
> An eight year long story of power and pride
> British Lord Vestey and Vincent Lingiari
> Were opposite men on opposite sides
> Vestey was fat with money and muscle
> Beef was his business, broad was his door
> Vincent was lean and spoke very little
> He had no bank balance, hard dirt was his floor

From little things big things grow song by Kev Carmody and Paul Kelly, first played by 'Paul Kelly and the messengers' in 1991

The Gurindji strike also known as the Wave Hill walk-off, took place on August 23rd 1966. Two hundred stockmen, domestic workers and families walked off Wave Hill Station (Kalkarindji). In 1975 they were officially granted a 30-year pastoral lease to a tract of traditional land. This was a landmark event in the struggle for Aboriginal land rights in Australia. The two songs cited above are well-known protest songs commemorating this affair. One written while the Gurindji were fighting for their rights and the second to celebrate the beginning of a long road to reconciliation and justice. There are books and papers written about the Gurindji of Dagurugu, the story has been told often. Frank Hardy's book, *The Unlucky Australians,* published in 1968, was the first major telling of this story and received wide attention. This chapter is one part of the story, how a group in South Australia organised a support group that followed the struggle through the years.

From the time of the Gurindji walk-off Roy and Don were donating money to the Northern Territory Council for Aboriginal Rights (NTCAR) to support the group. By November of 1966 Roy had set up the Heathcote Friends group and there are receipts from that year among Don's Gurindji papers signed by Davis Daniels as the secretary of the NTCAR. Dexter Daniels of the North Australian Workers Union (NAWU) was the president of NTCAR and Doug White the treasurer. The unions, especially people like Brian Manning of the Waterside Workers Federation (WWF) and Robert Tudawali of Actors Equity, actively campaigned towards supporting the Gurindji effort.

Roy died in 1968, the year after the 1967 referendum on the Aboriginal population being counted as part of the census and the Commonwealth having jurisdiction to make laws covering Aboriginal people. After Roy's death Don continued to have contact with Don McLeod in West Australia before going to Nigeria for a year in 1970. Returning to Adelaide the support for the Gurindji campaign was strong, especially in the eastern states and the Northern Territory. The paperwork on the Flinders University group actively working for the Gurindji cause starts after Don returned from Nigeria in 1971. He had campaigned for the 1967 referendum and all family members were scattered around our suburb handing out 'how-to-votes'. With the Wave Hill walk out Don was aware of the significance of what was happening and this was a view shared with Don McLeod. In a letter to Barrie Dexter, Secretary for Aboriginal Affairs under Gough Whitlam, McLeod expressed his opinion of what had been happening under successive governments.

> Apart from ourselves (the Nomad Group at Strelley) I suppose Wattie Creek is the only other independent group of Blackfellows in Australia and this must be crushed as we must be crushed before your policy of dragging Blackfellows down to the level of a white man can have any possibility of success.

The connection between the Nomads at Strelley and the Gurindji at Wattie Creek was maintained throughout the years the Gurindji were struggling for their land. Don arranged for Dr Bob Lloyd, a physics graduate from Flinders University, to go to Strelley to work with the Nomads[3] in early 1973. When Don McLeod wrote, "I think the need of the people [at Wattie Creek] are more deserving than ours"[4] Don would have been impressed at this generosity. Another PhD graduate from the Flinders University Physics Department, Phil Nitschke, decided to work at Wattie Creek and Don formally refereed him for a position where he would establish a garden for the camp as a source of fresh food. Phil would go on to become the field worker at the camp.

Don's serious engagement in the Gurindji land rights struggle started when he returned from Nigeria. He established the Flinders support group for the Gurindji quickly and in 1971 was seeking permission to visit Daguragu. Through his acquaintance, Jean Leu of the Save the Gurindji Campaign (SGC) in Sydney, he organised an introduction for the Flinders group with Vincent Lingiari and other Gurindji leaders. He threw himself into the struggle, visiting the Gurindji with two engineer friends to see what the Flinders group could offer. Over the next four years he made numerous visits. Three official ones when he was flown to the Northern Territory by the government and a number of trips that he financed himself in a small suburban car not suited to the terrain. I went with him on one of the 1972 trips and my brother accompanied him at least twice. Vic Barnett, who was secretary of the Flinders Gurindji support group visited with Don and also undertook trips to Daguragu separately. The Flinders University Physics Department link to the Gurindji fight was strong. Vic and Don were the office bearers of the Gurindji support group which changed its focus as needs changed. Bob Lloyd was at Strelley in 1973 with Don McLeod while at the same time Phil Nitschke went to work at Daguragu, first to establish a garden and shortly after he took up that position he was asked to become the field officer for the Gurindji group. Bob and Phil had been part of a group that Don worked and drank with at the Tonsley Pub. This hotel was a place where politics and long-term relationships were established and conversations at the Tonsley were mentioned fondly by both Bob and Phil in letters to Don. There were plenty of others who were part of the Tonsley crowd and this venue seems to have played a part in building connections among a number of activists. Interests ranged from Aboriginal struggles, to liveable cities, unions, politics and alternative energy. Phil Nitschke would become known for his support for the cause of euthanasia in Australia and the establishment of Exit International which has branches across Australian states.

Getting to Daguragu was no easy feat back in the early 1970s. The map below indicates how to get to the camp. As money was always tight Don would usually drive. Up to Katherine and then turn left towards the West Australian border. The Gurindji would only allow selected visitors and the place was very isolated. No telephone, the nearest settlement was Kalkarindji and that created problems as the Northern Territory Government had put money into building up this settlement at Wave Hill to try to entice the Gurindji to leave their humpies by the river and move to greater comfort at Kalkarindji. Various public servants, like the welfare officer, the local police and the government employment officer often worked against the idea of the Gurindji staying at Daguragu. Lyn Riddett, who spent about a year at Daguragu between 1970 and 1973 recalls some of the efforts the Wave Hill settlement people made to undermine the Gurindji campers. In a paper in *Labour History* in 1997 she recalls some of the tricks played. At the time she was in the camp the Gurindji had no transport so a settlement bus would pick the children up to take them to the school at Kalkarindji. Come evening the bus would not always return and it might be a few days before the children were brought home. The parents were assured they were safe because they were farmed out among extended family for the time they were held at the settlement.

For Don one issue was the post office. Letters and telegrams were the lifeline for those working with the Gurindji. The Gurindji elders were not literate and difficult legal matters were being negotiated as part of their claim to their land. Groups in the south needed to co-ordinate the support measures that were in place. For years the Gurindji were assisted by field officers like Phil Nitschke or his predecessor, David Quin, to keep records, pay accounts, read letters and transcribe replies, mend machinery and liaise with government bodies. The position of the field officer was funded through intermittent grants from the government while groups like ABSCHOL or Don's Flinders group, would pick up the tab if grants were late or tied up in red tape. During the time that Don was visiting Daguragu and raising money for the camp, there were often severe impediments to the level of communication supported by government officials. By the time Phil took over the field officer position there was reasonable suspicion that one welfare officer was not handing over precious letters in a timely way and was also probably reading them. As the Gurindji field officer, Phil had conflicts with post office staff so they refused to send on telegrams. This action was extended to include other supporters of the Gurindji. Don had telegrams sent to him while he was visiting the camp but they never arrived and he did not learn of their existence until he returned to Adelaide. Don put in an official complaint about telegrams not being delivered. The ensuing investigation found nothing and even tried to assert had the missing telegrams had never existed. The people at Daguragu therefore had to be vigilant about getting their mail, at one time organising their own mail bag but there were always difficulties. Face-to-face visits were essential to find out what was happening and what help was most needed.

As can be seen from the map below getting to Daguragu was part of the challenge. Don had called on Jean Leu of the SGC to organise his first trip in February 1971. On this visit he was accompanied by two colleagues, one who had considerable experience working in arid conditions so they would be self-sufficient in their travels. When the car arrived back in Adelaide after that trip it pulled into the street with a large plastic container of petrol strapped to the roof and a tube leading down into the engine. The car had landed in a huge patch of bulldust and the petrol tank had been smashed. The engineers fixed it as best they could and limped home. On the one occasion I went with Don, one of his 1972 trips, the car tyres kept bursting. We had spares but ran out short of William Creek on the way home. Hitch hiking into William Creek Don rang the police in Maree to try to arrange another wheel to be sent out. The police said, "Not many cars going west at this time of year" and I heard Don reply, "Then a police car will have to go west". We went back to the car and camped and next morning a police car arrived. They gave us the bill to settle with a garage in Maree on our way through. One other travel story. In 1974 Don had taken my brother David with him to Wattie Creek and David had managed to catch chicken pox. Don had organised with someone going through to Katherine to take him to Katherine so he could fly home. Not having money Don had sent a messsage to Daphne to transfer money for a plane ticket for David to the post office in Katherine. I drove Daphne to Adelaide airport on the day David was expected but he wasn't on the plane. We went home and came back to meet the next plane. Still no David. Daphne sat down and said, "I am not leaving the airport until he is home". Lucky he was on the next plane but his spots were very obvious and the airline steward looking after this spotty, unaccompanied minor was keeping her distance.

A letter from one of the women at Daguragu expressed concern for David going off on his own to Katherine when he wasn't well. Elsie Mayowie wrote:

> Muluga (Gurindji for old man) how are you goin mate, me Elsie saying hello and missus belong to you, she alright fella too.
> We mob bin worry for your little David along the plane, all picaninny like that fella. We look after you blokes proper way at Wattie Creek, good ones.

The letter is dated February 1974 and was transcribed by Jenny who had gone to Daguragu with Phil. From a number of letters I have that were written to Don by Gurindji elders the process was to transcribe a letter as accurately as possible so as to conserve nuance and meaning. What I notice most about the Gurindji letters I have on file is that the business part comes first and acknowledgements and social chat follows. Elsie's concern for David follows a letter to Daphne requesting cloth and sewing materials.

Achieving things at Daguragu could be slow. After the walk off there was the 1967 referendum and much publicity. The Liberal Party were still in government and the McMahon government passed a bill in 1972 opposing the idea of independent ownership of traditional lands and allowing only for long term leases. It looked as if it was going to be a long struggle. One of the issues the Adelaide group took up was the concern for the nutritional status of many of the Gurindji, especially the children. The Gurindji were isolated, depending on outside help to live and the problem of fresh food was even more difficult than in many other places in the Northern Territory. It was decided the Flinders Gurindji supporters would go to Daguragu to consult about setting up a garden project to supply fresh produce. It was for the garden project that Phil and Jenny went to Daguragu initially. The garden would require a good water supply throughout the year. As early as 1970 concern for a stable and sufficient water supply was raised by ABSCHOL. The reply from J.M. Hall for W. Angliss & Co. on November 23rd assured ABSCHOL that "the Government are making arrangements for drinking water for the Wattie Creek camp and therefore the question of a bore in that locality is not a matter of urgency".

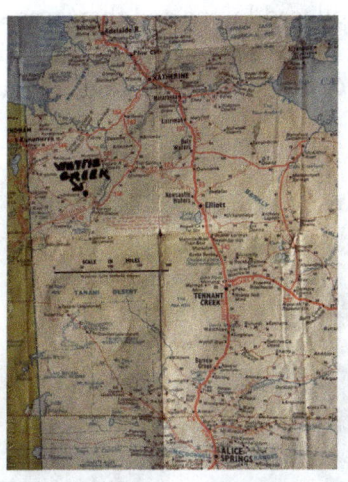

Figure 10.1 Map of the Northern Territory showing Wattie Creek. Don would drive to Katherine and then head west towards West Australia

In a letter cited in the Gurindji Campaign newsletter of November 1971[5], Jean Culley, who had been visiting the Gurindji from Melbourne noted how positive the garden was looking but there were water problems. She said there were problems with the supply of water as the river was getting low and she had heard that other areas, where bore water was available, had been waiting for two years for heads on their bores. The same year Rob Wesley-Smith, agronomist, activist, friend of the Gurindji, drew up a report on "Future possibilities at Wattie Creek".[6] He identified why the Gurindji should be supported, the importance of their resistance to government and the welfare branch of government. He commented on the aims of the struggle which emphasised the validity of the Gurindji claim, the right to community and self-respect and to help the Gurindji achieve the things they desired. He listed possible sources of income and one of these was agriculture. It was arguments like this that led the Flinders group to consult with the Gurindji and set up two funds, the garden fund and the stock fund. The stock fund was central to those in Adelaide organising for Lupna Giari (Captain Major) to visit Adelaide and address a number of public meetings in 1972. The largest meeting was at the SA Institute of Teachers Building in Parkside on 11th October. Don introduced Lupna and there was standing room only. Individuals and organisations gave generously and the Adelaide people were able to help the Gurindji acquire cattle, its own stock brand and branding irons.

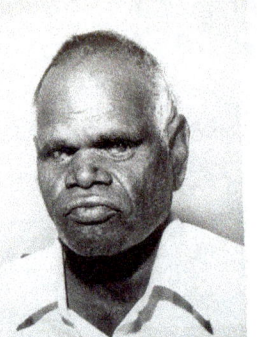 

Figure 10.2 Lupna Giari photo taken when he stayed in Adelaide with Don and Daphne. The portrait was drawn by the artist Herb McClintock[7] and was given to Don

In the report that Wesley-Smith had prepared he was able, as an agronomist, to detail the water supply that would be needed to develop a garden, the types of crops and the time of year when particular vegetables and fruits could be grown. On the question of bores, he said;

> Two bores have been drilled just upstream of Wattie Creek settlement and piped to Wave Hill settlement. As these bores tap the same basic source of water that supplies the Wattie Creek springs,

it is only reasonable that a share of their output be available to the settlement for their agricultural needs, as well as the vital one of domestic requirements.

Years of lobbying followed. The water and garden issue are just one example of how the Gurindji had to stand firm in the face of adverse actions from all levels of government and their representatives, right down to the local post-office, police and welfare officers. The fight for something as basic as a water supply went backwards and forwards for years. 1972 was the big year for letters about water supplies as the Flinders Gurindji Garden Fund was to be launched the following year and could not go ahead without a stable water supply.

Don was secretary of the Flinders University garden fund group and Vic Barnett was the treasurer. In this capacity they approached Ralph Jacobi, Labor Party member for the seat of Hawker and asked Jacobi to assist in trying to solve the water problem at Daguragu so the garden project could be properly activated. Ralph Jacobi proved to be a strong supporter and there was a flurry of letters[8] from May to August that year. Ralph Jacobi attempted to get some commitment about water supply from the Federal Liberal government. Ralph Hunt was the Minister for the Interior and the head of the National Party. Ralph Hunt acknowledged that the government knew there was a water supply problem at Wattie Creek during the dry season and would eventually provide a pipeline from the new bores built at the Wave Hill settlement. By July Ralph Jacobi had sent several letters to Hunt and spoken to him on the telephone. Ralph Jacobi sent Vic Barnett a written report on the telephone conversation. At this stage Hunt said the government had put the project of the pipeline from Wave Hill to Wattie Creek up for selective tender and work would begin by the end of the month. On the same day, July 7th, Hunt put out a press release stating that the Wave Hill settlement should have additional bores by the end of the year. A week later Hunt wrote to Jacobi stating that preliminary tests had been completed and the project was now in the hands of the Department of Works who would be the constructing authority. He could not guarantee that this would be included in the 1972-1973 works program for the Northern Territory. Vic Barnett wrote to Hunt telling him the situation was urgent, could not wait for another year or two and Gurindji supporters from Adelaide would try to do something about the problem.

This started a spate of letters to newspapers and other public forums and on July 21st Ralph Jacobi announced he would lead a team of 12 Flinders University technical and academic staff to lay on water supplies for Wattie Creek[9] and called on the Federal Government to pay for equipment. If the government would not provide the monies needed he would approach the state government and community groups to bear the cost. The Adelaide group publicised the Gurindji water difficulties as widely as possible. Don wrote to the editors of *Ondit* (Adelaide University student newspaper), *National U* (National Union of Students) and *The Review* in Melbourne. Daphne had a letter published in the letters page of *The Advertiser* on the 28th while Don had a letter in *The Australian* on the 31st. An answer to Don's letter (*The Australian*, 7th August) by the film-maker and journalist Cecil Holmes[10] was strong in its condemnation of the government delay. Cecil used words like "sinister", "subtle genocide" and suggested, "The denial of the most basic commodity – water – and at the same time the most easily available, makes this condition a crime rather than a scandal". Don and Cecil Holmes letters were responded to by N.W. Braidwood, director of public relations for the Department of the Interior who wrote to *The Australian* defending the government. Vic Barnett was having none of it (*The Australian*, 28th August) and gave his own response to Braidwood. Vic outlined where he agreed with Braidwood but went on to identify discrepancies in the government story and provided background. Part of the context was how governments at all levels were pouring money and services into the Wave Hill settlement to try to tempt Gurindji to leave their camp and move into the welfare town. He also explained that it was now the dry season and the garden and agricultural projects at Wattie Creek had been abandoned for the year and most of the inhabitants had been forced to leave.

By 1973 regular contributions were asked for the Flinders garden fund and they received a large number of willing donors. A pamphlet explained why the Flinders group had agreed to establish the project.[11]

> At Daguragu (Wattie Creek), the Gurindji have attempted to obtain some assistance for the development of a vegetable garden, in order

consciously to raise the level of nutrition amongst their own people. The Department of Aboriginal Affairs has agreed to support the scheme but has allowed one bureaucratic delay after another to hold up the allotment of the promised aid. The aid asked for by the Gurindji was to cover the salary of a garden worker specially selected at their request by their friends in Adelaide, irrigation equipment, plants, fertiliser and tools. Owing to these delays and the continuing low nutritional standard particularly of the children, it is now imperative that the Gurindji receive direct financial assistance from those of us who realise the hypocrisy and the prevailing Watergate level of morality amongst our bureaucrats.

The letter was signed by Don as secretary and Vic Barnett, as treasurer, added a slip for people to forward their pledges to the garden fund. Monies raised were intended to support Phil and Jenni in their work on establishing a viable supply of fresh vegetables at a level decided by the Gurindji. This situation changed later in the year when Phil accepted the role of field officer after the previous field officer, David Quin, had departed. In January 1974 the garden project had to be wound down as the department had not provided seeds, hoses, fertiliser, implements or any of the basic necessities for building a garden. The Flinders group were now worried about taking a regular pledge from people to support a garden when it wasn't progressing. They issued a new pamphlet and asked people to continue to make donations to the Gurindji "until we can get the bureaucracy moving and supply funds ... we are requesting some form of donation from time to time." The money would go directly to the Gurindji to help eradicate malnutrition. From February 1974 Jenny reported that Donald Nangiari, Pincher Numiari and three other Gurindji were entrusted with the garden and she was one of the workers. She thought the garden would be underway shortly. In June of 1974 Pincher[12] commented that the water installation needed attention:

> Now we got proper piping here; we been talking to welfare bloke in settlement to come here and help us fix this piping turn out. He never do it, still leaking after three months – it's a big mess. We try to get gravel because water lying around everywhere – lot of in Wattie

Creek. But they don't give we truck – we can do them job, but they got to give we truck.

The above quote is taken from a letter Pincher wrote in 1974 in respect to difficulties and complaints arising from government and welfare activities at Daguragu that had resulted in a visit from Rex Cavanagh as the Labor Minister for Aboriginal Affairs and Barrie Dexter, Director of Aboriginal Affairs. The complaints had been submitted to the government by various players including Vincent Lingiari and Phil, as the field officer. Daphne had started making notes for a letter campaign and it seems she had 10 grievances to be covered in 3 letters. The Sydney and Melbourne support groups had also received Phil's reports and were aware that minimal services to Daguragu had been halted and there had been various acts of chicanery by the local police and welfare officer and it was decided a delegation should go from the south to investigate some of the complaints coming from Daguragu.

Don was the representative from the south to be invited to visit the camp with Senator Cavanagh and Barrie Dexter and after the visit he submitted an alternative report.[13] He listed points that had been explored during the visit and his proposed recommendations for follow up. The issues addressed were land rights, a suitable pastoral manager for the Wattie Creek community, lack of co-operation for everyday services by the welfare officer, unemployment benefits and a number of complaints about the local police officer. The land rights claim was the major issue raised by Vincent Lingiari and although both Cavanagh and Dexter agreed the community needed their own land if they were to be self-governing the land might take time to acquire. Don suggested that an officer from the Department of Aboriginal Affairs should shortly visit Daguragu, finalise exact details of required land and forward details to Vincent Lingiari and Jean Leu. Jean Leu, of the SGC, should be part of the process as she had assisted with the initial land rights claim. Regular progress reports should be sent to Vincent Lingiari.

The question of the pastoral manager was a scandal. A pastoral manager had been appointed to the Gurindji without consulting the group. There was a feeling among the Gurindji supporters that the person 'chosen' did not necessarily have the Gurindji interests at heart.

Jean Leu wrote to Senator Cavanagh about this situation.

> I gather Mr (the welfare officer) had several discussions with the Gurindji about accepting S.S. (proposed pastoral manager) at Daguragu. Do you know who initiated this idea? With due respect, it appears that one or more persons is attempting to foist S.S. onto the Gurindji, who suspect him of representing the interests of the pastoralists in the area.

Jean Leu collected statements from the senior Gurindji men at Daguragu expressing their unhappiness with the appointment of this pastoral manager. On the question of a suitable pastoral manager all the southern support parties agreed that imposing a person without adequate consultation with stakeholders (the Gurindji) was not appropriate. To try to convince the Gurindji the local policeman and S.S. himself had gone to the Gurindji camp with copious amounts of alcohol and tried to win the Gurindji approval for the move. On that night the field officer, Phil and his father were both threatened by these outsiders. Bringing alcohol to the camp (which was dry) by the policeman to try to influence people to support the appointment of S.S. was considered reprehensible by both Cavanagh and Dexter. The threats to the field officer were the subject of a letter campaign. Letters condemning the threats were written by many supporters including Rob Oke of ABSCHOL in Melbourne, Don McLeod at Strelley and Don in Adelaide.

The question of unemployment benefits was not agreed by the delegation. Don argued on moral grounds that the Gurindji, in the absence of a grant to develop a self-supportive community should receive unemployment to continue their work at Daguragu as neither the welfare officer or Katherine employment officer, had offered concrete alternative employment. Information on employment had been submitted by Pincher Numiari who considered the denial of unemployment benefits "an attempt to force the Gurindji to work on other distant properties against their own interests."[12] There are employment forms in Don's files denying unemployment benefits for particular people. The assistant welfare officer had denied requests for unemployment stating there were jobs available. These forms were dated at a time when the welfare officer was away in Darwin. To add further concerns at least one of the men named on one of the forms in Don's files made a statement on record that he had not put his cross on the application form containing his name.

The police officer had been the subject of a number of complaints. Apart from bringing alcohol into the camp, which was condemned by the delegation, he had supported his wife in tricking Mick Rangiari into selling a horse for $40.00 that the Gurindji had just paid $120.00 for. A car, owned by the policeman, which was not suitable for the terrain and with mechanical problems was sold to Donald Nangiari who had recently received monies owed to him. The Gurindji did not make the accusations about the policeman in regards the horse and the car very forcibly to the visitors and Senator Cavanagh and Barrie Dexter deemed them not illegal even though the horse belonged to the company and not to Mick Rangiari. Don said the Gurindji later complained strongly about the policeman to him when he met with the local group in the camp round house. He wondered if this discrepancy may have been due to "decades of psychological oppression". From Don's report and Pincher's letter it would appear the visit achieved little. The Senator and Director listened but did not hear and were not prepared to take any effective action on the complaints.

At the same time that the Flinders University group were helping with the campaign for the water supply to Daguragu they were rethinking how their support should be delivered. Aware of the disappointment of the Gurindji at the lack of government support Don had been to the camp for three weeks at the beginning of 1974. Philip was now the field officer and since the departure of David Quin Phil had been busy with the daily clerical work. Phil and Don sorted the Muramulla Gurindji Company records and devised a system so the Gurindji could take more direct responsibility. This trip also led to the Adelaide group re-organising the two funds they had set up. The aim was to enable the Gurindji to have control of all projects, the fund would be reinstituted as the Gurindji Fund and the contributions could be used to suit the needs of the Gurindji including cash when required to offset daily expenditure. Equipment urgently needed at this time included parts for the Bedford truck, canteen bags, horse shoes, more brands, horn saws, leather punches, stationery and a filing cabinet. The new Gurindji fund was seen as part of the continuing struggle. It was a move towards maintaining an independent position while honouring Gurindji desires. For Vincent Lingiari remaining at Wattie Creek was of ultimate importance. This was expressed at the bottom of the letters he dictated to supporters. He finished his letters with the phrase, "This is my home".[14] Pincher Numiari expressed the same wish while also stating, "We supposed to make the decision for us, they supposed to listen to we."[12]

Figure 10.3 Aerial view of Wattie Creek with an inset of Vincent Lingiari. Source: Aboriginal Land Fund Report 1974-1975

Publicity activities and fundraising continued in Adelaide. Supporters were varied from a young teachers' college student, Kerry Boyd, who organised a practicum at Wave Hill, to a tobacco company (they asked for their substantial donation to not be made public), to enthusiastic young activists and many more. One person sent $100.00 dollars as a donation stating he was, "a baker's assistant at Balfours. I slave daily for the capitalists. But my condition as a wage slave is nothing compared to the ruthless destruction and exploitation of the Aboriginal people". Vic Barnett was the treasurer and his comprehensive records still exist. Many of the records are mundane but some suggest he also had to pursue members of the group at times. One letter from Phil[15] at Wattie Creek starts:

> Dear Vic, I detect a note of anxiety in your letter that was included with the last cheque for $200.00 that was sent to Katherine for the Muramulla Gurindji Co. Your exact words were "for fuck sake send a receipt" and I'm now writing in an attempt to carry out your wishes.

This is followed by a full-page typed letter requesting more information about activities in Adelaide and a couple of paragraphs reporting on what was happening at Wattie Creek. On the back, totally separate from the main letter, Phil had typed, "Received from Bank of Adelaide, Flinders Uni Branch, the sum of $200.00 for the Muramulla Gurindji Co." Vic's attempts at keeping meticulous records tested his patience at times.

Letters to newspaper editors were a frequent task. A number of the committee undertook this task. Vic wrote reports for the *Campus News* and Don tried to cover the student movement writing articles for *Empire Times* (at Flinders), *Clenched Fist* and *Ondit*. Talks accompanied by slides were a popular activity. Invitations came from community, political, church, student and other groups. Unfortunately, the projector carousels with the slides in them have long since disappeared. As reported in chapter 6 Don and Vic were even suspended from their employment at Flinders University after showing slides to a group of students who were occupying the registry in 1974. When Gough Whitlam went to Daguragu to present a lease for the Gurindji land on in August 1975 the following message from the Flinders group was sent to Vincent Lingiari and others at Daguragu.

> Your friends in Adelaide will be thinking of you over the week-end when you obtain your lease. We will have a small party to celebrate your gain. Some of us would have liked to be with you at this time, but that will have to wait.
> Vic Barnett, myself and other Adelaide friends have sent the following message through the Department of Aboriginal Affairs.
> Congratulations to the Gurindji people for eight years of hard

struggle. Your enduring courage has forced the Government to grant you a cattle lease for a portion of your ancestral lands. We greet this concession with genuine pleasure that your persistent efforts in the face of extreme opposition from Vesteys and the Government has been at least partially successful. After many promises by Wentworth, Bryant, Cavanagh and Dexter you have reached a milestone. The Gurindji supporters in Adelaide will continue to support you in your struggle for restoration of the remainder of your tribal lands to be held under full Aboriginal title. Yours fraternally, D. Atkinson.

However, Don did go to the ceremony. There is a telegram in the files telling Don that the Gurindji had requested his presence at the ceremony and the deputy prime minister had approved his flight by RAAF aircraft to fly him to the Northern Territory. Don donned his suit and went with alacrity to witness the Gurindji accepting a pastoral lease from the Whitlam government on 16th August.

As suggested in the above message Vic and Don were aware the battle was far from over. The story of 'The Dismissal' is well known and in the *Gurindji Newsletter* number 5, written by Don and Vic in March 1976, they warned readers that the Fraser Government was planning cuts in essential Aboriginal services. The Minister for Aboriginal Affairs, R.I. Viner, made a statement about authorisation of funding for the Muramulla Gurindji Co. Pty. Ltd. but did not say how much would actually go to the Gurindji for their cattle station. There was a worry that there had been an explosion of white bureaucrats at the Wave Hill settlement since the cattle lease had been granted and their salaries might be taken from the station money. At the time of writing the 5th newsletter Vic and Don estimated this could be up to 48 salaries. This newsletter was a sign off for Vic and Don as Don was organising to go back to Nigeria and Vic was returning to England with his family. In the interim they announced information would be available from the Melbourne Gurindji group. Don continued to work for the cause until he left for Nigeria as the leaflet advertising an evening with the Aboriginal Advancement League (pictured below) attests. On this occasion Don was the support act for Bob Randall the Aboriginal activist and singer. Don would give a commentary on the Gurindji struggle accompanied by his slides.

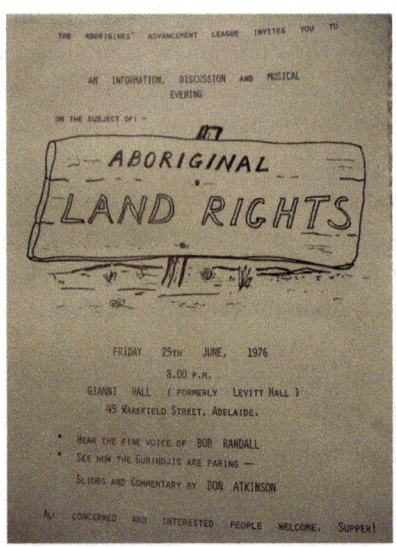

Figure 10.4 Aboriginal Advancement League invites people to an information and musical discussion 25th June 1976

In this chapter I have selected a few examples among the copious collection of letters, reports, records and newspaper articles that were associated with the Flinders Gurindji group and activities. The name Wattie Creek and Daguragu have been used depending on the label used in the letters or articles cited. Ralph Jacobi continued to support the Gurindji cause after the water pipes were realised. The pre-service teacher, Kerry Boyd, who went to Wave Hill was an active part of the Adelaide group. In 1975 she sent long letters back to Daphne and Don to inform the Adelaide organisation of activities at Wave Hill, including discussion of the draft legal papers for the coming lease. She had become interested and then an activist when she had experienced Bob Randall, singer and activist, teaching Aboriginal studies for the Torrens College of Advanced Education. She was interested in writing up the history of the of the Gurindji and their supporters and appealed to ABSCHOL in Melbourne for information prior to 1970. The reply to Kerry's letter, from Rob Oke, commended the idea of producing a history of Wattie Creek. He told her that although ABSCHOL had supported the Gurindji financially from the time of the walk-off most of their records were post-1969 as it was Christmas 1968 before an ABSCHOL person, David Twitt, was able to visit Wattie Creek. There is a similar gap in the papers I have on file. Receipts for donations to NTCAR as early as 1966 but the first activities and live meetings were not recorded until the beginning of 1971. Frank Hardy's account in *The Unlucky Australians* and newspaper reports have been the main source of information for the early years of the struggle though studies are growing.[16]

Travelling through the Northern Territory in 1972 I saw horrific examples of apartheid treatment of Aboriginal people. In one town we pulled into the local police station to collect water. The police station had a cell for white people and a cage outside for Aboriginal people. One town seemed to have a totally segregated main street. Vic and Don shared their home contact details in their newsletters and some dreadful letters were sent to Daphne and Don personally. One was handwritten and signed by "Anti-coon". Daphne did not know what to do with the letter and sent it to the editor of *The Australian* where the letter was quoted verbatim. There is no record of a response. Many people think the Gurindji struggle finished in 1975 but it was not until 1986 that they actually received freehold title to Daruragu Station. The Gurindji story is an important part of our history and is still unfolding today. At the same time the fight for land rights and human rights for Aboriginal people continues.

Figure 10.5 The author at Daguragu in 1972. I slept in the single women's quarters and these are two of the young women I shared the tent with

Chapter 11 Post university days

This chapter covers Don's activities when he returned from Nigeria for the last time. His mother, Annie, was preparing to move to Adelaide and would live just up the road from Don for ten years before needing extra care. The major informants for this part of the story have been Kim, my brother-in-law and Margaret, my sister. They were in Adelaide throughout Don's post university days and often worked with him or in close proximity on a number of enterprises and schemes that were pursued. Margaret was on the editorial committee of the magazine they launched in 1985. Kim and Don had two companies registered together. Margaret was also part of these initiatives. Don's most long-standing company was Atkinson and Associates. MMA was a company where the three, Kim, Don and Margaret officially joined forces. Five of Don's business cards are illustrated below (Figure 11.3). Kim and Don shared technical expertise and a love of working with their hands.

When Daphne and Don finally decided not to go back to Nigeria they actively started thinking about what they would do in Australia. They were both keen to write and wanted to share their experiences and interests in people and events across the world. The first idea was to set up a magazine, a Pacific Rim and Indian Ocean newscan that would collect material from radio and satellite. Don needed an aerial and the council area they lived in would not approve an aerial the height he was proposing. I lived on the other side of town in the inner western suburbs where the council would let him build his aerial. We arranged a house swap, the aerial was installed and Don set up receiving equipment. *Parandion* was born and they started publishing in February 1985.

Parandion was a family affair. Mum was the editor, my sister, Margaret, who had substantial office management experience, was the administrator and Don was in charge of the engineering. A friend, D. Kabruk, collected material in Zaria, Northern Nigeria. The list of countries monitored was impressive. Note: country names listed in their 1985 form.

Afghanistan, Australia, Bangladesh, Brunei, Burma, Canada, China (P.R.), China (Taiwan), Cook Islands, Ecuador, Ethiopia, Fiji (correspondent), Germany (F.R. Asian Service), Guam, India, Indonesia, Japan, Kampuchea, Kenya, Korea (D.R.), Korea (Rep.),

Malaysia, Marshall Islands, Micronesia, Nepal, New Zealand, Nigeria (correspondent), Pakistan, Papua New Guinea, Philippines, Singapore, Sri Lanka, Tanzania, Thailand, United Arab Emirates, United Kingdom (African and Asian Service), United Nations, U.S.A., U.S.S.R., Vanuatu, Vatican State (Asian Service), Vietnam.

Figure 11.1. The first copy of Parandion

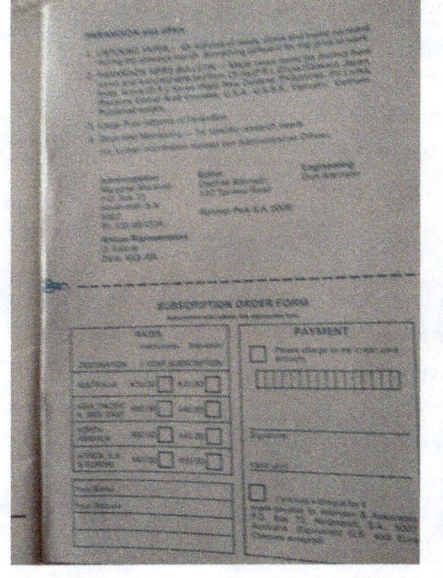 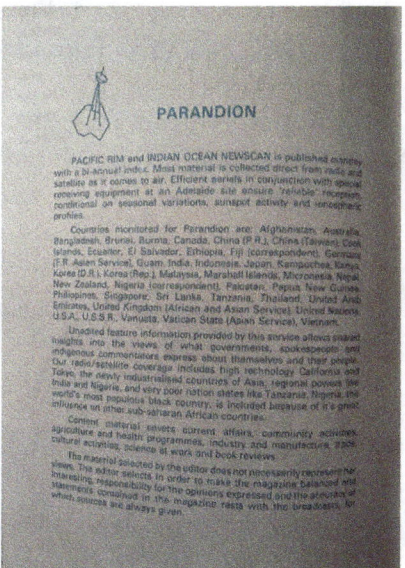

Figure 11.2. The inside covers of Parandion

In retrospect, this was an enormous task for three people to undertake at the time. Daphne went to college and learnt to use the new computer program, *Wordstar*.[1] Don set up the radio and recording system and they offered listening tapes, news bulletins, large-print editions and dedicated monitoring for researchers. Having the radio on almost constantly, especially at night for the different time zones meant Daphne and Don became used to the sound and for the rest of their days would have a radio on all night while they slept. My sister still has this habit. The sheer amount of information they collected, choosing material, transcribing and collating were time consuming undertakings. They offered monthly editions.

Certain topics were considered of more significance than others. There was a concerted effort to choose aspects of issues not covered in the mainstream media. From the first edition there was an emphasis on the "nuclear threat and the responsibility of scientists". An article in this first edition reported on part of an opening address at a Tokyo symposium 'On the nuclear threat'. To reference where the information was coming from Daphne listed, at the beginning of each article, the radio station, frequencies in kilohertz, the coordinated universal time and the date. For example, the Tokyo address on the article on the nuclear threat came from the radio station Japan N.H.K., 17810 kHz, 0175 U.T.C. on the 21st of February 1985.

In this first edition, there was news and commentary from a wide variety of places including Botswana, China (P.R.), Ethiopia and the Philippines. By March the nuclear arms race in space, Star Wars, was receiving attention. The discussion on the arms race was recorded from the American station U.S.A. – V.O.A. In April, Radio Moscow was talking Star Wars and military spending. Some articles were presumably chosen because they were interesting and on unusual topics. There was a discussion, in April, on the Voice of United Arab Emirates about Psychiatry in Dubai. An editorial decision to introduce two pages of 'catches' that consisted of small news articles that "were caught while monitoring feature programmes" was made in April. An early version of QI (Quite Interesting). These catches included such things as manioc (cassava) crisps being developed for the Fijian, New Zealand and Australian market, while another listed where the components of I.B.Ms personal computer (PC) parts were made suggesting it was a real 'world computer'. The keyboard, power supply and graphics printer came from Japan, most floppy disk drives were Singaporean, the monitor from Korea and semiconductors from the U.S., Japan and Far Eastern assembly plants. One of these 'catches 'reported on Australia's trade bureaucrats refusal to accept children's ballet shoes into Australia from the Cook Islands under the South Pacific Trade and Economic Cooperation Agreement (SPARTECA). These inexpensive shoes were available only in New Zealand and were the Cook Islands third biggest export. The report came from Radio New Zealand and Daphne's headline was, "Cook Island ballet shoes can't dance for Australia".

A lot of work went into producing these magazines. Sadly, many of the articles would still be newsworthy today as the world problems that attracted Daphne and Don, like the nuclear issue, are still issues. There was favourable feedback from subscribers, some asking for more information on particular topics, some made minor suggestions about formatting which were generally accepted. By the end of the first year, the magazine had attracted its first advertisers. One was *Arena*, the Australian Marxist journal and another, towards the end of the year, was for an Invasion day diary. Subscribers asked for background information on specific themes. The editor, or in the case of the example below, the engineer, would find further information to print or supply a lift-out. One of the lift-outs described below.

> Some subscribers have asked for background information on the Strategic Defence Initiative proposal. We had intended seeking permission to republish an article from *Electronics Today International* (ETI) before we came across this American information sheet. The Union of Concerned Scientists was only too happy for us to reprint their briefing paper. Engr. D. A. Atkinson

The lift-out is missing from the copy of the magazine I have. There were not enough subscribers and *Parandion* could not keep going. Daphne and Don would have embraced the technology of 2023 with the myriad news and commentary channels on the internet. *Parandion* is like an embryonic version of some of the shows available today on youtube, rumble or substack. They might have even got into podcasts. They would have been able to find a niche, exploit their particular interests and be part of a loose collective of left-wing journalists around the world.

While *Parandion* was in production it was marketed through 'Atkinson and Associates', one of the companies set up by Don. There were five different business cards in his files. From the addresses and names on the cards they seem to have been registered in the following order; 1, Atkinson & Associates, 2, Tesla-Farad, 3, Faraday Research, 4, Pancake Motor Company, 5, IEMS (Intelligent Electric Motor Solutions Pty. Ltd), where his card suggests he was registered as a consultant. He also had the company MMA with Kim and Margaret. Some of these companies would amount to taking out an ABN to act as a sole trader, often working as a consultant, while others entailed more. *Parandion* would have required processes for organising and distributing a magazine that would have needed registrations and copyright obligations. *Parandion* was the first major initiative that Don embarked upon after he had resigned from Ahmadu Bello University.

An important issue for Don was securing an income. Daphne nursed until she was sixty-five and then retired. She did not drink, but had been a heavy smoker for most of her adult life. When she decided to retire, she gave up smoking as she thought it was too expensive a habit to maintain once she was no longer earning. She was a bit annoyed that it took Don three weeks to notice she was not smoking. She never took it up again. Don turned his hand to a variety of jobs and different schemes. As early as 1979 he designed a science kit for schools. This was in-between contracts at Ahmadu Bello University. He had a contract to supply, for him, a large contingent of the kits to the Victorian Education Department. Members of the family helped solder the circuit boards over the Christmas holidays. He drove the kits to Victoria himself and they were delivered just in time for him to honour the contract.

He worked for the emergency housing office for a while doing electrical repairs. He formed a working partnership with an engineer friend who had worked at Phillips Electrical Industries until it was sold in 1980. Phillips at Hendon was the Australian headquarters of the company, the country's largest producer of electronic components and a major centre of technological skills and research. Phillips offered Don's friend, also called Don, a job in Victoria but he declined. Don Tonkin worked with both Don and Kim. He was a good friend and they enjoyed working with him except for a habit he had of cutting off cables a bit too short so as not to waste the wire. This made the job difficult at times. The three worked well together. Don Tonkin shared Don's interests in Australian history, literature and landscape and was the author of a biography about Hedley Herbert Finlayson[2] who was a mammologist with a profound interest in Australian mammals. The two Dons even did some house wiring, mainly for friends, but Don's days of climbing into ceilings were numbered.

Figure 11.3. Five business cards

Atkinson & Associates was Don's first company and the science kits for schools and *Parandion* came out under the Atkinson and Associates label. Atkinson and Associates may have been registered when Don and Bob Lloyd were working together on the electric car project. They had plans to do electrical design work together. This did not happen as the electric car project lost funding, Don went to Nigeria and Bob Lloyd went to work at the University of the South Pacific. Bob later set up his own company and consultancy[3] in Dunedin when he took a position at Otago University.

Kim became part of Atkinson and Associates and they also established MMA between Kim, Don and my sister Margaret. Don now concentrated on initiatives with Kim. These included designing parts for wheelchairs and completing discrete wheelchair repairs. Don's wheelchair involvement included motor design, research on batteries and chargers as well as electronic repairs. Don consulted on many and various things including high voltage power supplies and high efficiency motors. One anecdote remembered was that at one stage the Spastic Centre asked Don to design and build a controller for a train set for children with limited hand movement. The woman at the centre, who ordered the controller said, "'and make sure you charge plenty because when we want something else it would be good if your company was still in business". At the same time, Don was accepting contracts from Flinders University. The reports below are examples of contracts with Flinders University that Atkinson and Associates carried out over the course of 1990 - 1991. One project had a focus on different methods of charging batteries while the other focused on storage and batteries.

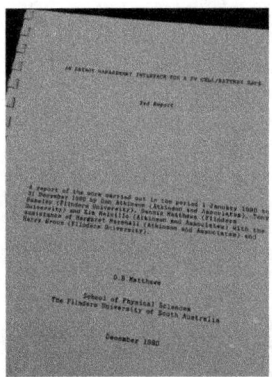 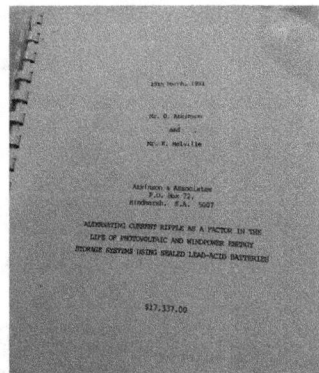

Figure 11.4. The first report was prepared by long-time friend and collaborator Dennis Matthews and the second by Atkinson & Associates

Don and Kim were partners in a number of electronic projects and collaborated with friends and extensive contacts they built up through their work activities. A main focus, built through word-of-mouth and then reputation was working with wheelchairs. Don liaised with an Australian company that built its wheelchair production from one wheelchair a week to one hundred per month. Don did some planning with this company on how to improve its product. Don was now exploring the idea of brushless motors and the manager of the company was attracted to the concept. The company also investigated the possibility of adapting a washing machine engine for a wheelchair. The idea of using a Fisher and

Paykel washing machine motor was explored. An important contribution was made through the battery research. Batteries in wheelchairs were a problem. In the 1990s, most batteries were still 'wet batteries' which meant they contained a liquid electrolyte such as sulphuric acid, battery acid. The batteries were problematic as they needed to be properly vented and had to always be in an upright position. These batteries would become less effective over time and there was always the risk of fire. The alternative being phased in was a sealed lead acid battery. Don and Kim conducted research on these sealed lead batteries specifically for wheelchairs. This was a neglected area. The other alternative, lithium ion batteries that have been around and researched for a long time have only, in recent years, been developed in relation to their potential for wheelchair users.[4]

The 1970s, electric car research that Don had convened had a strong emphasis on batteries. This long-term knowledge gave Don and Kim an advantage in the area of battery research when working with clients with specific needs. Back in the 1970s the battery used in the electric car was a lead acid (wet) battery and tests were directed at running speed of a motor together with battery current. The 1970s solution designed by Darryl Whitford was "to use a form of torque conversion between a constant R.P.M. shunt type printed circuit motor and the rear wheels".[5] The team focused on the vehicle operating with the minimum amount of power and the control system (the battery/motor relationship) having a minimum amount of loss. This early approach to looking at the batteries as a significant part of the equation was a foundation for future research and important for the effective use of wheelchairs. By the 1990s, when Don and Kim were playing with wet and dry battery technology there was also a renewed interest in vanadium batteries. Battery technology, as the need for effective storage grows is an ever-changing field. Many of the issues to be solved are familiar. The Chinese are now experimenting with replacing lithium ion with sodium ion batteries. Don would have been fascinated.

Another change that occurred to impact on the work being done by MMA was the restructuring of domiciliary care services in the Adelaide western suburbs. Initially there had been four centres each with specialist staff and their own workshops. A restructure saw the combining of the four workshops into one large workshop. This change resulted in times for repairs becoming longer and there was less attention allowed for targeted repairs for clients with specific needs. Don and Kim had established a reputation in addressing individual needs promptly so hospitals and care centres that supplied services for particular populations would approach them to assist with their electronic repairs. This meant there was a steady flow of incoming work.

Don was ready to help anyone who wanted assistance with creative work. Phil Nitschke approached Don for help with one of his 'suicide' machines. Phil's reminiscence:

> Thinking of the time I asked for Don's help developing an automated gas control device I was having trouble with. I'd planned to demonstrate it to a group of end of life activists, the so-called NuTech assisted suicide group, in San Francisco in 2003, but I couldn't get the prototype to work.
> Running out of time I asked Don for help. While intrigued with the idea of an automated device to control the gas flow in a plastic bag hypoxic death, I remember him expressing some reservation. This was not over any concern re assisted suicide, but rather he saw the idea as an unnecessary complication of a simple process. Despite this, he suggested and sourced some critical components and after a number of visits to Torrens Rd, the shoe box size device finally functioned.
> But, as it turned out he was correct. Technology for the sake of technology, with little practical benefit. Largely ignored by the NuTech gathering it was soon relegated to a shelf in the cupboard of failed ideas where it remained for years. Interestingly, I found it only this month when clearing out my Darwin workshop and I thought of Don and the help he offered, when the device was finally discarded (1/5/2023).

One of Don's community activities brought him back in touch with young people. He became an engineer in residence at Windsor Gardens Vocational College. He visited the college one day per week and the main thrust of his work at the college was to work with the students on the South Australian pedal prix. The business card for Don Atkinson, Pancake Motors (pictured above) was designed for this initiative. The pedal prix is an annual event in South Australia that started in 1986. The first pedal prix, at the University of South Australia was described as "a ragtag collection of home-built machines resembling bike-wheeled bedspreads".[6] The Windsor Gardens school wanted to encourage students to make things by learning about construction and design. The initiative was described as science meets technology. Today the pedal prix attracts more than 500 teams, 35,000 spectators and the race itself is conducted from Murray Bridge. Students in years 8-12 can join a pedal prix team. They learn to maintain, test and modify pedal powered vehicles. Schools can compete against each other.

When Don first joined the school at Windsor Gardens he helped the students explore all types of technology. One early experience was driving his car into the school grounds, lifting the bonnet and discussing the engine and the workings of the car. As he said afterwards some of the young ones were like the 'bush mechanics' on the television show. Some could start a car without a key almost by looking at it. He said he knew the mechanics of the car but it would take him ages to connect all the right wires to get a result. My sister remembered this story when she locked herself out of her car one day. She had got out of her car, taken her baby from the car seat (luckily) and slammed the door, locking her keys inside. A lad was walking past and she asked him if he knew how to get into a locked car. He was polite, obliging, pleased to help and opened the car quickly.

Hands on explorations of how things worked followed the car discussions. After this Don moved onto electric motors and started exploring motors for bikes. He may even have integrated his interest in washing machine motors for wheelchairs into motors for bikes. His projects at the school led to the Windsor Gardens team making their annual trip to the pedal prix. Each year the aim of the enterprise was to form a team, design and build a motor and enter the annual pedal prix competition. Each year Don would patent the design just in case the school could make some money from their efforts. The pedal prix was something that Daphne and Don were excited about and tried to persuade other people to watch at least part of it.

The Windsor Gardens Vocational College was given a Vocational Education Award one year. This award was for the work Don Atkinson had done. He would often talk about the school, his conversations with the Head. This was a project that gave him a lot of pleasure. Subsequently, two students from the school ended up working with Don on his last initiative with Intelligent Electric Motor Solutions Pty Ltd (IEMS) at Hindmarsh. The two young people, a male and a female, were working in the IEMS workshop when Don died. They attended his funeral. Don worked as a consultant to IEMS and as an entity it still exists and has a number of patents and partnerships advertised on the home page.[6]

When the Adelaide University Physics Department decided to invest in two high voltage power supplies Don was consulted on the design and building of this apparatus. They were DC power supplies with lots of current, big values like 80,000 volts. These large power supplies were rare at the time. There were two in the US, one in Canberra and Adelaide University thought this move would be a way of enabling researchers and students to carry out extensive experiments. Kim and a representative from Adelaide University went to Canberra to investigate their high volt power supply. As well as the information Adelaide University was seeking about the power supplies Don gave Kim an extra list of questions to pursue in Canberra. This was evidence of his thorough approach to investigating new situations. Adelaide was so pleased with their power supplies they decided to invest in two more a couple of years later. Although Don was at the periphery of this story it is an indication of the respect the scientists at the university had for Don's technical engineering skills. He knew many of the scientists at Adelaide University from when he first arrived in Adelaide and initially working at Adelaide University. This was for six months until the Flinders laboratories were completed and Flinders became an independent university under a state act. Don was familiar with the Adelaide department years before the consultation on the power supplies he was still being invited to collaborate on relevant projects. This ongoing relationship was an enabler for his final research initiative.

Brushless motors were the major theme among his interests in the 1990s. By the late 1990s, Don and Kim had developed a good D.C. brushless motor, they had focused on rotors, and the armature wiring and had built a motor that was 95% efficient. They were importing magnets from China that were stronger than the ones available from the U.S. It was time to think seriously about manufacturing. They were now interested in expanding. Don setup TeslaFarad while he and Kim also continued as Atkinson and Associates and MMA. They contacted possible investors for the motor and aimed to form a consortium. Two companies agreed to join the consortium. The brushless motors were to be built in Kim's workshop in River Street, Hindmarsh. Two extra people were employed and the companies in the partnership were to provide a monthly income for wages and materials.

This arrangement ran into trouble. One of the parties stopped paying their agreed instalments and sent aggressive letters to the other two companies involved. Those receiving the letters could make no sense of accusations being made against them. There was a suggestion that motor designs were being sold behind the complainants back. These letters continued for a while, followed by lawyers' letters and then a summons. There was a surmise that the man suing had run into money problems but the whole situation was never properly explained. The case was set for the Federal court. Don tried to get the court case moved to Adelaide but this was not possible. I was working in Melbourne at the time and attended the court case taking copious notes. The case was heard in the Federal Court before Judge Raymond Finkelstein. Don and the other defending company in Adelaide had their lawyers fly across to Melbourne for the big day. The complainant had lawyers in court but he was not present. The Judge did not seem to mind my taking notes so I made pages of notes that were as comprehensive as I could make them, writing by hand and given much of the much of the legal language was unfamiliar. The case was dismissed and costs were awarded against the complainant. I sent my notes to Don who said they contained lots of information not in the lawyers' reports. The court costs that had been awarded against the complainant but were never paid. This failure to pay costs is apparently, quite common. Don did not have the money to pursue his costs so that was the end of the affair. The court case was either in 1999 or 2000. Don returned to working on brushless motors.

The court case was a worrying time for Daphne and Don. The family had so little contact with law enforcement that Annie, at one stage, was disloyal to her son Don because of her fear of being involved with 'the law'. Don was pulled over in Adelaide for low-range drink driving. He had a NSW licence with his mother's address on it. He did this because his eyes were bad and he thought if he ever had to change his licence he might be required to have an eye test. He produced his licence for the Adelaide police and within days a telegram came from Sydney. Annie had written; "Sorry Don, told truth, said you hadn't lived here for twenty years. Scared of police. Mum". Don saw the funny side, changed his licence and had his licence suspended for three weeks. Mandatory laws would come later.

Don started working on a design for a brushless motor with the company, Intelligent Electric Motor Solutions (IEMS) who had the workspace in Hindmarsh. He now formed Faraday Consulting. It was here that the two young people from the Windsor Gardens Technical College were employed. This partnership was amicable and one night he rang my husband, Chris, to ask how university research grants worked. He said he had been away from Australian universities for so long he no longer knew the system. He said he had been working on rotors and had a design that he thought could fly. The company, IEMS, was willing to partner him in the development of the project. Chris told him to go to the University of Adelaide School of Electrical and Electronic Engineering, stand in the corridor and say, "I have an idea and an industry partner for a linkage application". Chris said they will come out of their offices running. I am not sure how Don approached the academics at the university but his design resulted in a Linkage ARC (Australian Research Council) grant.

He was working on the ARC almost up to the time he died. He had worked until the Christmas of 2006 and died in April 2007. A paper on the project was presented in Taiwan later that year. It was titled, *Analysis of a Segmented Brushless PM Machine Utilising Soft Magnetic Composites.*[6] The following appeared at the end of the paper.

ACKNOWLEDGMENT
This paper is dedicated to the co-author Don Atkinson who performed the initial design of the machine, but sadly passed away during the preparation of the paper.

The authors would like to thank the Australian Research Council (ARC Linkage Project: LP0455574) for supporting this project and the staff of the School of Electrical and Electronic Engineering's mechanical workshop for their help with the experimental testing.

The university went on to achieve another ARC grant based on this original research working with the same industry partner, IEMS. In 2014 Associate Professor Nesimi Ertugrul, the research leader for the two ARC grants described the work that the university and IEMS were doing.[7]

> In the developed world, more than 50% of all energy generated is used by electrical motors. This leaves a lot of room for efficiency gains.
> A significant portion of these motors are used to drive water pumps. They are invisible, but used everywhere - in pools, vehicles, boats, irrigation and industry. For example, large buildings have multiple water pumps and every swimming pool has at least one water pump which runs for several hours a day, consuming a large amount of electrical energy."
> The University of Adelaide researchers have used two emerging magnetic materials - called soft magnetic composite (SMC) and amorphous magnetic material (AMM) - and two novel production techniques to form the 'stator' within the electrical motor or generator. The stator is the stationary and magnetic part of a motor surrounding the rotor which turns.
> Using SMC material and working with industry partner Intelligent Electric Motor Solutions (IEMS) Pty Ltd, the researchers have developed motors that operate at low speed with high power output and with low production costs, suitable for swimming pool and similar pumps.
> The research teams have developed patented prototypes, using both technologies, and testing facilities and are now looking for further investment partners to commercialise the technology.
> The research has been funded through two different Australian Research Council linkage project grants.

The IEMS company has also stayed the distance. On the website the company states;[8]

> IEMS is a technology company involved in innovation, design and manufacturing of small-scale, high-power density and high-efficiency Brushless Permanent Magnet motors and generators utilizing soft magnet composites (SMC).

They acknowledge their partnership with the University of Adelaide while describing other activities of the company. By 2016 they had patents in the US and in 2021 added China and Europe to the places they had patents. Don could not know how the idea would be taken up and grow. He was pleased to have the ARC grant at the end of his working days, he enjoyed working at the IEMS workshop so he finished work on a good note.

Paid and volunteer undertakings were not the only interest Don had in his post university years. He had a workshop cum office in the backyard at his home and this was known as the Gunyah. The Gunyah was a corrugated iron shed painted a dark green. It was lined and was an L shape. The Gunyah could not be seen from the back door as Daphne and Don liked to grow trees and other plants in great profusion. Daphne had a theory that everyone should plant and look after 80 trees across their life to make up for what they took from the atmosphere. She put this into practice and had continual fights with the local council as she even grew trees on the median strip and tried to prevent them being pruned. There were some lively fights but while she was there in the house she usually won. The Gunyah was set up like an office and a workshop. There was a desk, computer, printer and photocopier, beer fridge and coffee-making material in one part of the L shape and the longer part of the structure was a workshop and storeroom with filing cabinets. Many hours were spent in the Gunyah and there were precious collections in the filing cabinets. One of these collections was Don's copies of *Electronics Australia.*

This journal reflected many of the things Don was enthusiastic about. *Electronics Australia* was an Australian magazine that was published from 1922 -2000. In 1922 it was known as the *Wireless Weekly*. In 1939 it was renamed *Radio Hobbies*, becoming more technical and including build-your-own kits aimed at hobbyists. In 1955 television was added and the magazine was again renamed, this time becoming *Radio, Television and Hobbies*. Changes in the world of science, growing fields of knowledge like computing and medical technology brought another change in 1965 when the magazine became *Electronics Australia*. The last edition appeared in March 2000. This publication was everything Don liked. It was Australian, it emphasised technical explanations of how things worked and the how-to-build kits represented an aim to educate everyday Australians on how to make and understand electronics.

The how-to-build projects were popular. I remember in the early 1960s being given a kit to build a transistor radio. This was a complete kit and all the resources needed were sent out in one package. The radio was a wonderful thing. It came with a pale blue plastic case that would be vintage aesthetic today. I put the radio together and Don checked it and got it to work. My soldering was neat but not always effective. One particularly popular DIY project was published in 1979, across a number of editions of the magazine. This was the DREAM – 6800.[8] The DREAM was described, "as a ridiculously simple hobby computer with 2K bites of memory that played game programs on a TV". What was not to love.

Don had a collection of the magazine that looked complete. He had subscribed for most of his adult life and had carefully saved all editions. When he was in Nigeria he would get frustrated because his subscriptions often did not arrive. When he returned to Australia he would chase up the missing copies. One reason for this collection, though he valued *Electronics Australia* for its own sake was to use it as a foundation for a history of Australian electrical engineering in the twentieth century, especially after the second-world-war. This was an on-going interest and at the end when he realised he would not have time to achieve this he was regretful as he did not know anyone who would take his collection and write up the history he had always wanted to see.

This is a Cook's tour through some of Don's engineering activities and plans in his post university life. I finish the chapter with an image of Don and a windmill in the 1950s.

Figure 11.5 Don and windmill 1950s

Chapter 12 – the book case at the end of the life

This chapter winds up my story of Don Atkinson, radical engineer. He was 80 when he died of mesothelioma. Still engaged in his research work until the end and his interest in technology was unabated. In the last few weeks he no longer listened to the radio each night but audible books of Dick Francis novels. From this action I take the theme for this final chapter. The bookcase at the end of the life. As a Marxist Don saw literature and reading of same as more than personal pleasure and as an expression of the social and political conditions of the time. Of the act of reading Freire has said:

> The question of the importance of reading is addressed by considering the ways in which experience itself is read through the interaction of the self and the world. Through examining memories of childhood, it is possible to view objects and experiences as texts, words, and letters and to see growing awareness of the world as a kind of reading through which the self learns and changes. The actual act of reading literary texts is seen as part of a wider process of human development and growth based on understanding both one's own experience and the social world. Learning to read must be seen as an aspect of the act of knowing and as a creative act. Reading the world thus precedes reading the word and writing a new text must be seen as one way of transforming the world.[1]

Books were rare in Australian working-class homes in 1927 when Don was born. Visiting his childhood home in the 1950's I remember one small bookcase in the hallway with possibly ten books. The only one I remember was, *A House is Built,* by Barnard Eldershaw. This novel was about a Royal Navy officer who set up a business in Sydney in 1837. It won the *The Bulletin* prize in 1928. An interest in Australiana was something my grandparents shared as both had ancestors living in the colony at the time the Barnard Eldershaw book was set. I do not know if Don ever read the Barnard Eldershaw book. He certainly would later read *Coonardoo* by Katherine Susannah Pritchard that shared *The Bulletin* prize with *A House is Built* in 1928. Katherine Susannah Pritchard was an important spokesperson for the Australian left and a founding member of the Communist Party. *Coonardoo* is an early exploration of a white Australian family on a station and the relationship between the son Hughie and the Indigenous girl of the title, Coonardoo. This was a brave book but it was a book of its time so a lot of the language, characterisations and the plot are now unacceptable. Don's parents, Annie and David, were unlikely to have read a controversial book that portrayed interracial sexuality. Don would possibly have agreed with Jacqueline Wright's[2] summing up of the book who found *Coonardoo* an uncomfortable read but a significant piece of Australian literature.

> To me, *Coonardoo* is more than a book that captures the deep-seated prejudice of white Australia through an exposé of interracial sexuality. It's a milestone marking a shift in thinking, and a pleasant reminder of how literature can challenge and change perceptions and stereotypes.

Don's copy of *The Children's Treasure House* was mentioned in chapter, 2 as a special childhood possession. He also told the family that his favourite books growing up were the William books, by Richmal Crompton and *Swallows and Amazons* by Arthur Ransome. The two series are still part of the canon of childhood today. Don's enjoyment of these two series were passed on to the next two generations of the family so they belong on the bookcase. William was a scruffy non-conformist, forever eleven years-old. He is frequently described as an anti-hero, his speech patterns are working class and his appeal to children is that he is always in trouble but a good, moral child underneath. William is gentle, middle-class comedy. *Swallows and Amazons* is less well known.

Malcolm Muggeridge reviewed *Swallows and Amazons* in *The Manchester Guardian* in 1930. He thought the very charm of the book lay in the fact that these were ordinary children.

> ... the book is the very stuff of play. It is make-believe such as all children have indulged in: even children who have not been so fortunate as to have a lake and a boat and an island but only a backyard amongst the semis of Suburbia.

This taste in the gentle and comedic remained and could be seen in books Don read across his life. He loved Clochmerle,[3] a book that is a satirical take on conflict between Catholics and Republicans in a small French village. In the 1950's he embraced the *Little World of Don Camillo*[4] set in rural Italy after world-war-11. In the Po Valley the ex-partisan priest, Don Camillo, struggles with the communist mayor, Peppone. Closer to home a favourite Australian comic writer was Lennie Lower. *Here's Luck* and *The Best of Lennie Lower* are sitting together on the bookcase. The last book he ever read was by Alexander McCall-Smith, *44 Scotland Street*. The family were not sure if he had quite finished it and we knew he was really enjoying it so we threw it into the coffin just in case.

Leaving school at fifteen and starting an apprenticeship was the beginning of Don including less mainstream literature in his reading. He was introduced to politics while completing his apprenticeship at Braybon Brothers and at this time had his first experience of activism by participating in a campaign for daytime training for apprentices. During the war compromises were made to meet industrial needs but by the end of the war the unions wanted to see improved wages and conditions. By the time he met Daphne Don was well-versed in left literature and had developed an enthusiasm for Australiana, especially working-class history and fiction, much of it through the Australasian Book Society (ABS). There were other left book clubs/societies around the world at the time and samples from a number were in Don's collection. Progress Publishers were established in Moscow in 1931. This was an important propaganda arm of the Soviet Union and made the works of luminaries of the left, like Marx, Engels and Lenin available in English at an affordable cost to young workers like my father. Among the books from Moscow on the bookcase, apart from the compulsory volumes of *Capital*, was a copy of *Selected Works* by I. P. Pavlov. This edition, published in 1955, by the 'Foreign languages publishing house' combined politics and science and therefore catered to Don's main interests. Another book club was the Left Book Club set up in England by Victor Gollancz in 1936. The Left Book Club lasted until 1957 and at one stage had 57,000 members. There were many of these books on Don's shelves with their plain red covers and the statement, "not for sale to the public" at the bottom of the front. Many of the book club books Don kept on his shelves were published before the war. Don was too young to have been interested in these books in the 1930s but he was fascinated with the rise of Nazi Germany and how it had been enabled. Presumably these early books were bought through the party bookshop in Sydney or at one of the second-hand bookshops he loved. One of the books was a copy of Clifford Odets play, *Waiting for Lefty* (1935) which was performed by the Sydney New Theatre in 1936. Edgar Snow's *Red star over China: the rise of the red army* (1937) was an important book for the left as it was the only account, in English, of Mao Zedong and the Chinese Communist party at this time. For this reason, it has retained its historical importance and been reprinted many times.

Another book club represented on the bookcase was the Readers Union Ltd. J.M. Dent and Sons founded the Phoenix Book Company in 1928 to sell books on the instalment plan and in 1937 this became the Readers Union. Once again, books were only available to members. The Readers Union books were sourced from a variety of publishers based on their quality and members would pay a fixed amount each month for a book. Among the books from the Readers Union that Don had in his collection were Stephen Spender's *World Within World* (1953) and books by Aldous Huxley (1954) and Bertrand Russell (1958). Time payment, the "never-never", was a popular way of gaining credit in the 1950's. While we were in Armidale, 1957 – 1964, Don bought the Encyclopaedia Britannica on time payment. The encyclopaedia also provided annual updates. The encyclopaedia proved to be a white elephant but he bought it with the best of intentions.

By the time Don met Daphne he had started his own book collection. One of the first Australian books he acquired was a first edition of *The Glugs of Gosh* by C. J. Dennis. He revelled in the language, but was concerned with overtones of nationalism, protectionism and anti-immigration ideas held by many Labour people, including C.J. Dennis, at the time. The following description of the Glugs when they engaged in free trade with the Ogs is an example of clever and appealing language, the shirts especially, but the underlying message is anti-Chinese.

> So the Glugs continued, with greed and glee,
> To buy cheap clothing, and pills, and tea;

Till every Glug in the land of Gosh
Owned three clean shirts and a fourth in the wash.
But they all grew idle, and fond of ease,
And easy to swindle, and hard to please.

Throughout his life, Don liked things made in Australia and grieved as the country lost much of the manufacturing sector. As members of the ABS Don and Daphne actively supported the organisation, especially entertaining authors in Armidale. The ABS was an important project. The book club was registered in 1952. The aim was to produce four books per year for a new group of readers by new writers. This was a cold war cultural initiative. The co-operative was established as a social progress initiative and targeted a literary working-class readership. The collection of ABS books on Don's shelf was almost complete with only three volumes missing. Social realism was a prevailing literary trend and this was the genre promoted by the ABS. Don's interest in Australian literature extended to history and poetry. Looking across the bookcase I see two history volumes that were cherished. One of the books is *Our Yesterdays: Australian Life since 1853 in Photographs*. The volume *Our Yesterdays* was 'arranged' by Irma Pearl and Cyril Pearl supplied a commentary. First published in 1954 the commentary is insightful, reflecting popular tastes of the time. Cyril Pearl carefully researched the subjects. An example:

Figure 12.2. *The communard Michael Seringue, p. 44.*

Cyril Pearl's commentary:

In April 1873 the French transport L'Orme put into Port Phillip, bound for the penal settlement at New Caledonia with political prisoners from the Paris Commune. One of them, a sailor called Michael Seringue, jumped overboard and made his way to Melbourne where he became, in the words of the 'Argus', 'the Communist hero of the day'. The 'Argus' published his life story, written by Marcus Clarke, and at Clarke's suggestion, opened a fund for him – 'not because he is an escaped Communist,' wrote Clarke, 'not because he has performed a daring athletic feat, but simply because he is a fellow creature, who without having done any great harm in this wondrous world … is now among us without English, without money, almost without friends.' This photograph is one of many taken by a Melbourne studio to meet public demand.

The *Our Yesterday* book was especially valuable as it was a goodbye present from the Parkers, a well-known communist family in Sydney, when the family moved to Canberra. A companion volume was a present to Don the same year. This book was *True Patriots All*, "garnered and decorated" by Geoffrey Ingleton (1952). *True Patriots All* is a collection of broadsides from the early days of the colony. These two books were unusual for the time and treasured.

Don and Daphne's enthusiasm for Australian literature coincided with the folklore revival and had similar underpinnings. The war was over, Australia was a different country, there was a growing feeling that the history of Australia consisted of more than Captain Cook, explorers, squatters and the Anzacs. Some Australian literature had emerged in the 19th century and Don was familiar with the likes of Marcus Clarke and Tom Collins. He had tried unsuccessfully to read Patrick White's '*Voss*' in the 1950's but now there was Australian literature emerging that reflected the country he knew. If the literature was subversive this added to its significance as there was plenty about Australia in the 1950's that felt socially and politically constraining. Don thoroughly enjoyed Alan Seymour's 1958 play *The One Day of the Year*. Growing up with the celebration of war, that in his opinion was a failed campaign that resulted in unnecessary human slaughter, he hated Anzac Day. He was thrilled when Alan Seymour's play appeared. Today it has lost some of its sting because the intergenerational differences explored in the play have become the main emphasis of the story and this has been at the expense of the focus of the particular (Anzac) day. Don lived long enough to see the Anzac parade begin to grow and successive governments pour huge amounts of money from the public purse into the war memorial. He had hoped he was living in a country where in the words of the singer/song writer, Eric Bogle, "Someday no one will march there at all"[4] would become a statement of fact.

By the 1960's Don had extended his interests beyond the folk revival of 1950s Australia. He still valued this literature but there were more books being published all the time, they were accessible and new ideas were being propagated. The 1960s saw a flowering of activist literature that was compatible with Don's world-view. Vance Packard's *The Waste Makers* was an early example. Published in 1960 it took aim at the consumer society and planned obsolescence. He enjoyed Betty Friedan's *The Feminine Mystique* (1963) and other similar works. One of the most influential on Don's thinking was James Baldwin's *The Fire Next time* (1963). This book was a savage indictment of race relations in America and helped confirm his strong opinions about racism in all its forms. He read the Black American literature avidly. Ralph Ellison's *Invisible Man* (1952) is there on the shelf along with Toni Morrison and Richard Wright's *Black Boy* (1945). One person who ticked all the boxes as a giant figure he admired was Paul Robeson. Don's interest in Robeson never abated and he considered no book case collection could ever be complete without a number of biographies about Robeson.

By the 60's Don was buying and reading a more eclectic collection of books. While the family was in Ghana acquisition of books changed. In Armidale a trip to the town library was a Saturday morning ritual and books were mainly bought as presents. In Ghana there was no similar lending library available but books were cheap compared to Australia. The family decided we would buy a book each per week and share our choices. *I Claudius* and *Claudius the God* by Robert Graves were two books bought at the university bookshop over a two-week period. The two books were enjoyed by the four older members of the family and became a particular favourite with Daphne. My older sister, Mayo, developed an enthusiasm for Doris Lessing at this time. She would go on to write her Masters Thesis on Lessing. This year in Africa taught us how lucky we were to have access to books and to share our tastes with others. It also taught us to be book buyers and by the time each of us left the family home we had a substantial bookcase of our own chosen books to take with us.

There was a poetry section on Don's bookcase. *The poetical works of Alfred, Lord Tennyson* (1910) was the oldest acquired outside of a second-hand shop. The Tennyson book was a prize my maternal grandmother had won at school. Other favourites came from the second-hand bookshops that Don would haunt. Browning and Shelley were two poets that Don and Daphne would recite to each other. Don's tastes were varied but he did have favourite themes. He had a record of A. D. Hope reading his own poems, recorded in 1972. As children of their era both Don and Daphne loved *The Rubaiyat* of Omar Khayyam. *The Rubaiyat* was cited at both their funerals. There were volumes of Henry Lawson and books about Lawson on the shelves. A prized collection from the early 1950s was *Freedom on the Wallaby: Poems of the Australian people* edited by Marjorie Pizer for the Pinchgut Press, Wharf Lane, Sydney. There is a bookmark on a page marking poems by Victor Daley. Don was attracted Daley and his lyrical Bohemian poetry with a feeling for humanity. Below is the last verse of the poem *Disillusion* that was on the page Don had marked.

> Give to me the grasp of true man,
> Though his state be high or low,
> Give to me the kiss of woman,
> Let your Seas and Forests go:
> There is nothing but the human
> Touch can heal the human woe (From *Freedom on the Wallaby*, p. 89)

First Australian's poetry had been on the shelf since the early party days. Oodgeru Noonuccal (Kath Walker) was the first as she was known in the communist world. She had joined the Realist Writers group who published her first poems. She was the first published Aboriginal poet and poems like *Son of Mine* are well-known and much cited. However, the hope for a better future that Oodgeru Noonuccal expressed in her 1964 anthology, which contained *Son of Mine* seems a long way from gaining fruition. Oodgeru Noonuccal remained an activist for the Aboriginal cause but became increasingly embittered as she observed an absence of any real change. Land rights seemed a long way off and she became more interested in self-determination. My father was sympathetic to Oodgeru Noonuccal's growing bitterness towards white Australia. Other well-known First Australian poets represented on the bookcase are Jack Davis, Kevin Gilbert and Lionel Fogarty.

Part of the collection that should not be left out were his love of murder mysteries. There were only a few examples on the bookcase as these were books he would read and pass on but he thoroughly enjoyed a good murder. The green Penguin crime books were favourites with writers like Josephine Tey, Raymond Chandler, Carter Dickson and Ngaio Marsh. Daphne and Don did not have a television until the 1980s so recorded music and books were staple entertainment in the evenings. Part of Saturday shopping at the Adelaide market was to visit the second-hand book stall in the market and stock up with light reading for the week. When finished they would pass the books on or return them to the book stall. Don also enjoyed science fiction in the same way. Reading authors like Isaac Asimov, Fred Hoyle, Kurt Vonnegut and John Wyndham. Towards the end of his life he got pleasure from listening to Dick Francis books.

It was at Braybon Brothers his interest in engineering and all things electric took form. Throughout Don's life he read technical papers and there are plenty of examples of drawings and designs in his files. His feelings for *Electronics Australia* have been described in chapter 11. His ideas about scientists and society were represented across the books he collected during the years. An early example was James Wilson's *Science and the progress of man*. This publication is mentioned in chapter 3 as Don cited Wilson in an essay he wrote in 1951.

He also started reading history and philosophy of science. '*The Origins of Modern Science*' by Herbert Butterfield (1968) was one excursion into this genre. Butterfield is now criticised for concentrating on the 'big picture' or for those who support a big picture approach the wrong 'big picture' but Don kept it on his bookcase so the book reflected a meaningful view of science for him. He was reading such books for pleasure by the late 1950s. It is also a measure of how he was becoming open to ideas that were not necessarily part of the left-wing canon. He would have possibly even admired Butterfield's strong religious approach to life, as he did not consider science and religion to be incompatible, while at the same time he was becoming sceptical about taking a western-centric approach to science. He could appreciate Kurt Mendelssohn's *Science and Western Domination* (1976) and love the machines he worked with while suspecting there were other views. He also had those he considered classics and books like *'Origin of the Species'* he considered essential reading and all the family were presented their own copies as presents. James Lovelock's work on the Gaia hypothesis he found fascinating.

Figure 12.3 James Wilson (1949). Science and the progress of man. Sydney: Current Book Distributors

World events were important. The dropping of the bombs on Japan at the end of World-War-11 had a profound effect. At a time when there was not a lot of general literature on this event Don read Bronowski's *'Science and Human Values.* Bronowski's three essays that make up the book start with an essay called "The creative mind". The idea for the book came to Bronowski as he stood in the desolate landscape of the bombed Nagasaki where "40,000 were killed by a flash which lasted seconds".

On an evening like that evening, some time in 1945, each of us in his own way learned that his imagination had been dwarfed.

Don managed to source other books on the bombing. An early one was, '*Hiroshima Diary: The Journal of a Japanese Physician, August 6 – September 30, 1945*. Later he would buy books like Kenzaburō Ōe's *Hiroshima Notes* (1965). A Japanese friend living in Adelaide asking to borrow these books because she had two high school children and she wanted to share this history with them. This would have been in the 1970s and she said such books were not easily available at the time. This general and philosophical interest in science continued all his life.

His interest in First Australian history and literature was strong from his early days in Sydney. Many books on this topic were on the shelf at the end of his life but were still mainly by white Australians. Books by anthropologists, the Berndts, in the in the 1950s, Roland Robinson's books of legends and dreaming plus Bill Harney's stories were all there. He kept up with the reviews and was actively seeking new authors like Tara June Winch and Alexis Wright whose works were just emerging in the years before his death. His attention went beyond people to the land itself and when he found a revised edition of Charles Laseron's *Ancient Australia* (1984) he couldn't resist it and placed it on the bookcase next to a tatty, well-read first edition from 1954. In 1976 he was obviously doing some research as I found three slips for interlibrary loan requests tucked inside his copy of Roland Robinson's *Black- feller, white feller* (1958). One slip for Alfred Searcy's *In Australian Tropics* published in 1907, the second was for J. M. Holmes *Australia's Open North* from 1966 and the third was a journal article by an R. Duncan on South Australia's contribution to the Northern Territory cattle industry. The Duncan article appeared in the journal *Historical Studies of Australia and New Zealand*. The three slips have library catalogue numbers next to them and he has filled out an account number for the photocopying of the article. I assume this research was to do with the Gurindji struggles.

After the time in Nigeria he added African writers to the selection. The poet and playwright Wole Soyinka was a favourite author and he possessed books and tapes of Soyinka's writings. His contemporary African library grew considerably after his years in Nigeria. This part of the chapter is largely missing as I do not have access to the vast collection of African writers on the bookcase. I most clearly remember earlier books on Africa that reflected his political approach to post-colonialism and led to his initial interest in Africa. He admired leaders like Kwame Nkrumah, Julius Nyere, Patrice Lamumba, Muammar Gaddafi and Robert Mugabe and had publications by them on the bookcase. Not all remained in the admired category and he became disillusioned with the likes of Robert Mugabe as the sad history of his reign in Zimbabwe played out. When he did go to Nigeria my sister commented on how thoroughly he researched the country. When Don died Daphne moved to a retirement village and their house was packed up. I took most of the Australiana, music and history books. My sister kept arts and literature material. My brother has the contemporary African library as he spent most years with Daphne and Don in Africa. These books are in storage in another state so I was not able to access them. The only reminder I have of the recent African part of the collection is a copy of Peter Godwin's memoir called *When a Crocodile Eats the Sun*. Don bought it for me after he had heard an interview on *Late Night Live* (LNL) and hoped the book would live up to the hype. This book was published in 2006 and is the memoir of a white person growing up in what was then Rhodesia. It was one of the last books he gave me.

The last section of the books on the shelf belong to a period when Don had a close customer relationship with a local bookseller. This phase existed for the last 12 years of life. A rather magical shop called 'Imprints'[5] moved to Adelaide, to Hindley Street. Don was good at sniffing out new bookshops, good restaurants and pubs where the jazz was all right so he quickly acquainted himself with 'Imprints' when it opened in Adelaide. The shop opened in 1984 and this year coincided with his return to Adelaide from Nigeria. On the website 'Imprints' is described as "the cultural cornerstone of Adelaide's west end" and "t[T] he quintessential modern bookshop". Don had found a bookshop in Adelaide he loved and all his books and books he bought as presents came from 'Imprints' during these twelve years. Initially he would go into the bookshop and browse. It is aesthetic and the atmosphere is great. Later, after his stroke, driving into the CBD and parking was more difficult so he started to order books. 'Imprints' gave Don a discount as a subscriber customer.

When they realised what a voracious reader he was they also instigated a service where one of the staff would pop past the house with his books when they came in. After Don's death Daphne was offered his discount but they could no longer offer personal delivery.

A quick look at the bookshelf contains the books Don chose to read in his last years and indicates an eclectic group with an underlying theme of an interest in people, the natural world and a curiosity on how things work. He also maintained a strong concern for politics and the state of the world. I have chosen a few from the shelf as examples of his interests in the final years. The first example is Zoltan Torey's *The Crucible of Consciousness* published in 1999. Zoltan Torey was a psychologist, a philosopher and a polymath. He left the Soviet Union (Hungary) in 1948 and arrived in Melbourne the following year. An accident in a battery plant blinded him in 1951 and this meant he attempted to see through a system he described as "internal visualisation". With this background Zoltan Torey set out to explore the conscious mind. In the summary of *The Crucible of Consciousness* Zoltan Torey comments on the mind as "living matter's processing epicentre in whose focus ambiguities are resolved… we may begin to sense that a dynamic quest may be in progress". Don would have thoroughly approved the ending of the book as Torey finishes by quoting Tennyson's Ulysses:

> but something ere the end,
> Some work of noble note, may yet be done,
> Not unbecoming men that strove with gods.
> The lights begin to twinkle from the rocks;
> The long day wanes; the slow moon climbs; the deep
> Moans round with many voices. Come, my friends,
> 'Tis not too late to seek a newer world

No list of books that Don enjoyed would be complete without a book by Stephen Jay Gould. Gould's enthusiasms and enormous output were precious to Don the reader. The only Gould example I can see among his books from the 'Imprints' days is a reprint of *Ever Since Darwin: Reflections in Natural History* from 1992. I cannot believe that he had not read this book in an earlier edition as Gould was a favourite from when his books first appeared in the 1970s. Don kept books and would reread them so an earlier edition had probably disappeared. He often lent his books and this one was important enough to need replacing. *Ever Since Darwin* is a series of essays that were originally published in the *Natural History Magazine*. The topics across the different sections and their titles are intriguing. For example, section six is titled, "Size and shape, from churches to brains to planets". The scope of the essays and their organisation makes great reading. Gould is a witty writer and Don would comment to the family that most of the bibliographic notes on the covers of his books seriously under estimated the man. That Gould and Richard Dawkins participated in heated and public debates about their views on evolution and the relationship between science and religion was a source of reading pleasure. Don always thought there was not enough meaningful discussion and robust argument, in the world of ideas.

Another book in the collection that bears the 'Imprints' sticker is Peter Galbraith's *The End of Iraq*. This book was first published in 2006 so it was bought the year before Don died when the armed conflict in Iraq was still raging. Saddam Hussein was executed in December 2006. Don had been distressed at the invasion, horrified at the 'shock and awe' campaign and the subsequent killing, especially of civilians, in Iraq. Galbraith's book outlines the flawed invasion and the spurious reasons given for the invasion. Galbraith discusses the mistakes the Americans made in planning what they thought would be a quick regime change. According to Galbraith one fatal problem was that the Americans had no Plan B. America did not extract itself from Iraq until 2011 and went back again in 2014. Don would not live to see these events but already with critics like Galbraith discussing the depth of America's incompetence and the idea of "the war without end" he would not have been surprised at how long America has been bogged down in Iraq.

In this chapter, I have tried to express the changes and growth that took place across my father's life. From the early favourites of childhood that championed adventure and non-conformity in a safe, moral context to his love of all things electronic and his explorations into literature and history, especially Australian. His adventures with reading, in the latter years, have been summarised with three examples of his dealings with the 'Imprints' bookshop. A scientific discussion of the mind, a loved book replaced and a current affairs book on the war in Iraq. Always a reader he read for light entertainment as well as for a love of learning and exploring challenging ideas. Books were company all his life. At the very end, struggling to breathe, he could still find energy to enjoy Dick Francis, one of his preferred mystery writers and McCall-Smith who was reminiscent of the early safety of the William books while also showing a refreshing take on surrounding events that have a hint of danger. When he died Don was in the living room surrounded by family and his books. The doctor had come that afternoon and shifted him to a hospital bed in the room. Lying flat on his back he became unresponsive and his breathing became loud and laboured. Kim wondered if the sound was a death rattle. The night nurse had arrived and suggested we should talk to him.

Notes

Chapter 1
Atkinson, D. & Gehlert, D. (Intelligent Electric Motor Solutions Pty. Ltd.) with Liew, G., Tsang, S., Ertugrul, N. & Soong, W. (University of Adelaide). (2007). Analysis of a segmented brushless PM machine utilising soft magnetic composites. *33rd Conference of the IEEE Industrial Electronics Society (IECON)*. Taipei. November 5 - 8

Snow, C.P. (1962). *Magnanimity: Rectorial address*. University of St Andrews Student Representative Council. http://14.139.58.199:8080/jspui/bitstream/123456789/1268/1/PH%20179.9%20S%2061%20M.pdf

Ward, C. (2016). *A handful of sand: The Gurindji struggle after the walk-off*. Monash University Press.

Riddett, L. (1997). The strike that became a land rights movement: a southern 'do-gooder' reflects on Wattie Creek 1966-74. *Labour History*. 20. Pp. 50-65.

Goode, E. (2001). A conversation with/ Oliver Sacks; Character forged by periodic table and family tree. *The New York Times*. December 4th https://www.nytimes.com/2001/12/04/science/conversation-with-oliver-sacks-character-forged-periodic-table-family-tree.html

Chapter 2
Radiola Deep Image television receiver https://collection.maas.museum/object/349166

Hygeia Dissolventor toilet https://collection.maas.museum/object/158676

Schmacher, E. (1973). *Small is beautiful. Economics as if people mattered*. Penguin Books.

Chapter 3
Ward, R. (1988). The price of liberty. In Franklin, M. *The New England Experience: Inside stories of U.N.E. 1938-1988*. Chapter 17. 167-177

Ward, R. (1980). Reminiscence. *The Australian University Degree*. 23(1). P. 53-54

Nura, Yunusa, (2016). Arewa knot (DAGIN AREWA): The origin. https://www.academia.edu/30465097/AREWA_KNOT_DAGIN_AREWA_THE_ORIGIN

Williams, G. (2010). *The communist party dissolution bill and its aftermath.* https://labourhistorycanberra.org/2015/05/the-communist-party-dissolution-bill-and-its-aftermath/

Schreker, E. (2004). McCarthyism: political repression and fear of communism. *Social Research: An International Quarterly.* 71(4). 1041-1086

Steve Nelson https://spartacus-educational.com/SPnelsonS.htm

Lennie Lower. Humourist. His most famous work and only novel *Here's Luck.* http://gutenberg.net.au/ebooks01/0100081.txt

Sparrow, J. (2012). A short history of Communist jazz. https://overland.org.au/2012/06/a-short-history-of-communist-jazz/

Enright, F. (1994). The illustrious life of Sydney's New Theatre. *Green Left.* Issue 138, 13th April. https://www.greenleft.org.au/content/illustrious-life-sydneys-new-theatre

Salisbury, S. (2012). Memories of Reedy River and the Bush Music Club https://www.labourhistory.org.au/hummer/the-hummer-vol-8-no-1-2012/reedyriver/

Palmer, H. *Birth of an old bush ballad.* http://members.optushome.com.au/spainter/Ballad.html

Peter Mason. A biography. https://adb.anu.edu.au/biography/mason-peter-14943

Chapter 4

Letters from J.M. Somerville 13th February and 11th March, 1957

Marsh, K. (2009). *Conversations with Australian scientists: Professor Robyn Stokes* https://www.science.org.au/learning/general-audience/history/interviews-australian-scientists/professor-robin-stokes-chemist#productivelab

Wendt, H. (2008). The contribution of the Division of Radiophysics Potts Hill and Murraybank field stations to international radio astronomy. PhD thesis. James Cook University. https://researchonline.jcu.edu.au/7995/1/01front.pdf

Fletcher, N. (2010). *Conversations with Australian scientists: Dr William Blevin.* https://www.science.org.au/learning/general-audience/history/interviews-australian-scientists/dr-william-blevin-applied

Personal recollections provided by Dr Herbert Stock

Letter from Kurt Landecker from Geneva 30th November, 1964

Landecker, K. (1961). *Means for the generation and transmission of very large frequency waves.* https://insight.rpxcorp.com/patent/US3011051A1

The legendary Ana Aslan Institute: The business story of its rejuvenation. (2018). *BR Business Review.* 5/5/2018 https://business-review.eu/news/the-legendary-ana-aslan-institute-the-business-story-of-its-rejuvenation-167775

Tullipan, R. Australian author https://adb.anu.edu.au/biography/tullipan-ronald-william-11890

Manifold, J. Australian poet, musicologist and writer https://mypoeticside.com/poets/john-streeter-manifold-poems

Gregory, M. (2008). *Australian folk songs: Edgar Waters 1925-2008* https://folkstream.com/edgarwaters.html

English, C. (1955). Letter from London October, Tuesday 25th.

China's cause is my cause: Rewi Alley's sixty years in China. *Global Times.* August 13th,2021 https://www.globaltimes.cn/page/202108/1231411.shtml#:~:text=Rewi%20Alley%20was%20one%20of,widely%20told%20on%20Chinese%20land.

Medgar Evers https://www.fbi.gov/history/famous-cases/medgar-evers

Chapter 5

Biney, B. (2007). *Kwame Nkrumah: An Intellectual Biography.* Thesis submitted for the degree of Doctor of Philosophy at the University of London. https://eprints.soas.ac.uk/28819/1/10672987.pdf

Padmore, G. (1936). *How Britain rules Africa.* New York: Lothrop, Lea and Shepard company.

Nkrumah, K. (1957). *The autobiography of Kwame Nkrumah.* T. Nelson, Edinburgh.

Harvey, W. (1966). *Law and social change in Ghana.* Princeton Legacy Library.

Fitch, R. & Oppenheimer, M. (1966). Ghana : End of an Illusion. *Monthly Review.* July-August 1966; Special Issue vol. 18, no.3.)

Chapter 6

Blake, A. (n.d.) *Physics in Adelaide:* https://set.adelaide.edu.au/physicalsciences/ua/media/1135/physics-in-adelaide-the-1960s.pdf

Rogers, W. (1961). The scientific revolution and adult education. *Australian Journal of Adult Education*, 1. 12-16.

Bramble, T. (1993). Trade union organization and workplace industrial relations in the vehicle industry 1963-1991. *Journal of Industrial Relations.* 35(1). 39-61

Arena magazine https://en.wikipedia.org/wiki/Arena_(Australian_publishing_co-operative)

Empire times Student newspaper at Flinders University established in 1969.

Lloyd, B. (2023). *100 years of insanity: nuclear war, climate change, peak oil, propaganda and the role of tyranny.* Dunedin: Raynbird Books.

Battle of Flinders turns sour https://trove.nla.gov.au/newspaper/article/110725992

Gadd, K. (2002). Supporting success: science technicians in schools and colleges. The Royal Society, London. https://royalsociety.org/~/media/royal_society_content/policy/publications/2002/9970.pdf

Chapter 7

Press release to *The Advertiser* 23rd April, 1974. "For release Monday 22nd April, 1974. Sent to Darryl Whitford for comment. Darryl was one of the original group of three working on the Flinders EV

Award for 'city car'. *The News.* Tuesday November 21st, 1972. P. 5

Hogg, T. (1968). Electrophant: Sheer audacity combined with superb engineering. *Road and Track.* April. Pp. 59-63

Video *Investigator Mark 1* https://www.youtube.com/watch?v=6cs8vAp3L28

Video *Bruce Tonkin explaining the restoration (conservation) of the Investigator Mark 1* https://www.youtube.com/watch?v=ftFztJ00A6o

Firms order prototypes of SA electric car. *The News.* Thursday November 19th, 1973. P. 5

Ford, T. (1973). Our electric car project featured at the Royal Show. *Flinders News.* August. 20.

News release 7th March, 1973. *Infoplan Ptd,Ltd.* New electric car concept – SA government to finance development

Atkinson, D. (1973). Flinders University electric vehicle project. *SA Science Teachers Journal.* 3. Pp. 18-21

Australian Information Service: News and Information Bureau. May 29th 1973. Australia develops new electric car. Story by Jonathan Stone and photography by Douglas McNaughton

On Campus. Friday April 26th, 1974. No. 80

Royal Automobile Association. *South Australian Motor.* 58(4). July 1st, 1975. Front cover and p.7

Kirby, J. (1976). Electric car in danger: Cut in funds. *Sunday Mail.* August 8th pp. 39 and 135

Resignation letter from Don Atkinson to The Registrar, Flinders University, August 2nd, 1976

Folley, C. (1979). Car of the future drives Darryl. *Sunday Mail.* August 5th, p. 23

Llewellen-Smith, M. (2012). *Behind the scenes: The politics of planning Adelaide.* University of Adelaide Press

Nick, G. (2021). When "can't-do capitalism" killed the Flinders electric vehicle project. *Vanguard.* November. https://cpaml.org/post4.php?id=2395

Bruce Tonkin. Email correspondence

Chapter 8

Atkinson D. *Jacob is Ku (The name is taken from a popular Nigerian-English television series).* Conference presentation given at Ahmadu Bello University. Date uncertain but post 1982

Wikipedia. *Timeline of Nigerian History.* https://en.wikipedia.org/wiki/Timeline_of_Nigerian_history#20th_century

Letter from Dr Mahmud Tukur to the acting Editor of "New Nigerian Newspapers Ltd. P.O. Box 254, Kaduna. October 10th 1981

Statement to the ASUU (Academic staff union of universities) branch of ABU (Ahmadu Bello University) by Dr George Kwanashie. October 14th 1981

Fatuyio, A. & Ologunwat, P. (n.d.) An evaluation of the state of ceramic industries in Nigeria. https://www.academia.edu/5391205/An_Evaluation_of_Ceramic_Industries_in_Nigeria

Gwadabe, M. (2010). Yosufu Bala Usman (1945"2005). *Africa.* February https://www.researchgate.net/publication/238606419_Yusufu_Bala_Usman_19452005

Chapter 9

New Deal for Aborigines – Tom Right https://www.marxists.org/history/international/comintern/sections/australia/1944/19440531.htm

Dick Roughsey https://adb.anu.edu.au/biography/roughsey-dickgoobalathaldin-14193

Tidd, G. (1972). *Thoughts and thought*. Sydney: Wentworth Books.

Nucleus – Letter to editor, p. 3. 4/6/63

Reverent Clint https://adb.anu.edu.au/biography/clint-william-alfred-9766#:~:text=William%20Alfred%20Clint%20(1906%2D1980,came%20to%20Sydney%20in%201910.

TRANBY https://tranby.edu.au/about-us/

Archives (Special List GRG52/900, p. 293. https://archives.sa.gov.au/sites/default/files/public/images/GRG52-90%20Special%20List%20for%20website.pdf

Report of union (BLF) delegation to Walgett 13th – 15th August 1965. Ray Peckham reported on Trade Union delegation which went to Walgett in 1964 to inquire into the jailing of 2 children

Dorothy Hewitt https://unionsong.com/u399.html

Film and protest meeting 1957 https://www.nma.gov.au/__data/assets/pdf_file/0011/692390/aboriginal-australian-fellowship-petition.pdf

Chapter 10

Gurindji Blues song written in 1969

From little things big things grow song by Kev Carmody and Paul Kelly The Nomads of West Australia https://www.monash.edu/__data/assets/pdf_file/0004/1671016/richardson-20-1.pdf

Letter from Don McLeod to Phil Nitschke about the garden for Wattie Creek

Gurindji Campaign Newsletter 21st October 1971

Wesley-Smith, R. (1971). *Report on the future possibilities of Wattie Creek*. October

Herb McClintock. Founding member of the Realist Artists in Sydney and a friend of Don https://adb.anu.edu.au/biography/mcclintock-herbert-15773

Letter from Hunt to Jacobi 24th May; Jacobi to Hunt 31st May; Jacobi to Hunt 19th June; Jacobi to Barnett 7th July; Press statement Hunt 7th July; Hunt to Jacobi 11th July, Barnett to Lingiari 17th July; Barnett to Jacobi 20th July.

They'll aid Aborigines. *The News*. Friday 21st July, p. 54

Cecil Homes remembered https://aso.gov.au/people/Cecil_Holmes/portrait/

Pamphlet to members from the Gurindji Garden Fund group in Adelaide

Letter from Pincher Numiari 5th June, 1974 to supporters generally. He was reporting on the fact finding visit by Cavanagh, Dexter and Don to the Gurindji camp.

Visit to Daguragu by Senator Cavanagh, Mr Dexter and Don Atkinson 29/5/74. Report and conclusions by Don Atkinson

There are three letters on file from Vincent Lingiari in 1974 and each one finishes with the phrase, "This is my home"

Letter to Vic Barnett from Phil Nitschke dated 17th August 1974

Ward, C. (2016). *A handful of sand.* Monash University Publishers

Chapter 11

The first word processing software program people could use on home computers. https://www.thoughtco.com/wordstar-the-first-word-processor-1992664

Tonkin, D. (2001). *A truly remarkable man: The life of H.H. Finlayson and his adventures in Western Australia.* Seaview Press.

Bob Lloyd consultancy*

Sunwoo, Yuk., Kiwon, Choi., Sang-Geon, Park. & Sukmin, Lee. (2019). A Study on the Reliability Test of a Lithium Battery in Medical Electric Wheelchairs for Vulnerable Drivers. *Applied Sciences.* 9, 2299. https://www.researchgate.net/publication/333639131_A_Study_on_the_Reliability_Test_of_a_Lithium_Battery_in_Medical_Electric_Wheelchairs_for_Vulnerable_Drivers/link/5cf866814585153c3db736d4/download

Atkinson, D. (1973). Flinders University electric car project. *South Australian Science Teachers Journal.* 733. 18-21

Atkinson, D., Gehlert, D., Liew, G., Tsang, E., Ertugrul, N. & Soong, W. (2007). Analysis of a Segmented Brushless PM Machine Utilising Soft Magnetic Composites. *The 33rd Annual Conference of the IEEE Industrial Electronics Society (IECON)* Nov. 5-8, 2007, Taipei, Taiwan

Adelaide University News (2014). Statement by Associate Professor Nesimi Ertugrul.

https://www.adelaide.edu.au/news/news71582.html

Intelligent electric motor solutions (iems). https://intelligentmotors.com.au/about-us/

Electronics Australia (1979). DREAM 6800 Archive Site. http://www.

mjbauer.biz/DREAM6800.htm

Chapter 12

Freire, P. (1981). The importance of the act of reading. *Journal of Education*. https://serendipstudio.org/exchange/files/freire.pdf

Wright, J. On 'Coonardoo' by Katherine Susannah Pritchard. *Griffith Review*. https://www.griffithreview.com/coonardoo-katharine-susannah-prichard/

Eric Bogle (1971). *The band played Waltzing Matilda.* https://www.google.com/search?q=eric+bogle+the+band+played+waltzing+matilda+lyrics&rlz=1C1GCEA_enAU799AU799&oq=Eric+Bogle&aqs=chrome.3.0i355i433i512j46i433i512j46i512j0i512l4j46i512j0i512j46i512.14932j0j7&sourceid=chrome&ie=UTF-8

Imprints bookshop https://imprints.com.au/

www.ingramcontent.com/pod-product-compliance
Lightning Source LLC
Chambersburg PA
CBHW070647160426
43194CB00009B/1611